JON COLLINS BLACK'S
There's
Treasure Inside

By

Brad Willian

Contents

Introduction:

The Greatest Treasure Hunt in American History

Welcome to the Treasure Hunt

You are about to embark on an unparalleled journey, one that promises not only the discovery of rare and valuable treasures but also an adventure that will take you through the annals of American history, the depths of personal growth, and the pursuit of the extraordinary. This is not just any treasure hunt—this is the ultimate quest, one that blends the excitement of a real-life search with the rich storytelling of history's most iconic figures and treasures.

Imagine yourself standing on the brink of uncovering a fortune worth millions of dollars, scattered across the United States, waiting for someone with the courage, the knowledge, and the persistence to find it. This treasure, unlike any other, is a collection of items as varied as they are invaluable: from rare Pokémon cards to shipwreck bounty, from Bitcoin to historical artifacts once owned by the likes of George Washington, Amelia Earhart, and Picasso. The treasure hunt you are about to undertake is a once-in-a-lifetime opportunity to connect the material with the meaningful, to explore both the past and the present, and to discover that the greatest treasures often lie not just in what is found, but in the journey itself.

The Story Behind *There's Treasure Inside*

The story of *There's Treasure Inside* begins with a single, bold statement: "I've hidden a treasure somewhere in the United States, and it's worth millions." This declaration is not just a challenge; it's an invitation to anyone willing to participate in the adventure of a lifetime. But this book is more than a treasure map; it's a guide that helps you understand the significance of the treasure you are searching for.

The treasures hidden within these pages are not just valuable for their worth in gold, Bitcoin, or artifacts. Each item is carefully chosen to appeal to a wide array of interests—from history enthusiasts to collectors, from the curious to the driven. There are rare collectibles that reflect the ever-evolving culture of America, pieces tied to legendary figures, and items with a deep historical connection. This treasure hunt goes beyond simply finding valuable objects—it's an exploration of how history, wealth, culture, and personal growth intersect.

Jon Collins-Black, the mastermind behind this treasure hunt, has crafted a story that connects you to the American landscape in a way you may never have experienced before. Through this journey, you will not only uncover treasures but will gain a deeper appreciation for the incredible people, moments, and movements that have shaped the nation.

How to Use This Book: Your Key to the Ultimate Treasure

To succeed in this treasure hunt, you must approach this book with an open mind and a keen sense of adventure. *There's Treasure Inside* is not a traditional narrative where the story unfolds in a linear fashion. Instead, this book is structured as a treasure map, a guide filled with clues, stories, and riddles that will lead you on your quest. Each chapter offers a key to unlocking a different treasure—some tangible, some intangible.

Here's how you can make the most of this unique experience:

1. **Read with Curiosity:** Every word and every story within these pages is a clue, a piece of the puzzle. As you delve into the historical context and personal anecdotes, keep your eyes peeled for subtle hints that might guide you toward the treasure.

2. **Engage with the Journey:** This is not just about finding riches. It's about embracing the adventure and the lessons learned along the way. As you progress, think of each treasure you discover as a stepping stone to greater understanding—whether it's about the history behind an artifact or the personal growth that comes from taking on such a monumental challenge.

3. **Decipher the Clues:** The treasure hunt is designed to test not just your ability to search, but your skill in decoding clues, solving riddles, and connecting dots across history. The clues are scattered throughout the book, often woven into the narrative. Pay attention to the smallest details, as the key to unlocking the next treasure could be hidden in plain sight.

4. **Embrace the Treasure Beyond Gold:** While material treasures are certainly part of this hunt, the true riches lie in the experience itself. The real reward is the growth, knowledge, and sense of accomplishment that will come from taking part in this journey.

Remember, this book is your ultimate guide and map. Every page turns into a step forward in your quest. By the end, whether you find literal treasure or not, you will be richer for having participated in this extraordinary journey.

The Hidden Treasure

What's Hidden and Where: An Overview of the Treasure

Hidden somewhere in the vast and varied landscapes of the United States is a treasure of immense value, both in its literal worth and in the legacy it represents. This treasure, curated with great care, is unlike any other—it spans centuries, cultures, and interests, creating a collection as diverse and fascinating as America itself. Worth millions and growing more valuable each day, it includes items that intrigue collectors, history buffs, and adventurers alike.

The treasure isn't confined to a single chest of gold or a vault of jewels. Instead, it is a mosaic of pieces that reflect the evolution of wealth, culture, and human achievement. The collection includes:

- **Bitcoin and cryptocurrency**, representing the cutting-edge digital economy.

- **Shipwreck artifacts**, offering a glimpse into the mysteries of the ocean's depths.

- **Rare collectibles**, such as Pokémon cards and sports memorabilia, connecting to modern culture.

- **Historical artifacts**, including items owned by legends like George Washington, Amelia Earhart, and Pablo Picasso.

- **Gold and precious metals**, timeless symbols of wealth and security.

- **Rare gems and antiquities**, each with its own story to tell.

The exact locations of these treasures remain a mystery, as they are scattered across the United States. Some may lie hidden in forests, deserts, or mountains, while others might be tucked away in plain sight, waiting for a keen observer to uncover them. Each clue and hint in this book will guide you closer to these remarkable finds, but the journey will require more than luck. It will demand curiosity, critical thinking, and a willingness to explore.

The treasures are designed not only to reward the finder with material wealth but also to spark a connection to the stories and histories they represent. Whether you are drawn to the cutting-edge allure of Bitcoin or the timeless elegance of a rare gem, each piece contributes to a larger narrative of discovery, adventure, and the endless pursuit of treasure.

Bitcoin and Cryptocurrency: The Future of Wealth

Among the treasures hidden in this great hunt is Bitcoin, a revolutionary form of digital currency that has transformed how we think about money. Unlike gold or physical collectibles, Bitcoin exists entirely in the digital realm, representing the cutting edge of modern financial systems. Its inclusion in the treasure highlights the blending of old and new, showing how the concept of wealth evolves over time.

Why Bitcoin Matters in the Treasure Hunt

Bitcoin is more than just a valuable asset—it symbolizes the democratization of wealth. Unlike traditional currencies controlled by governments and banks, Bitcoin operates on a decentralized network called blockchain. This innovation makes it resistant to manipulation and inflation, ensuring its value as a long-term investment. As you embark on this treasure hunt, discovering Bitcoin isn't just about financial gain; it's about connecting to the future of technology and economy.

The Role of Cryptocurrency in Wealth Building

Cryptocurrencies like Bitcoin have gained immense popularity in recent years due to their potential for high returns and their ability to bypass traditional financial systems. By including Bitcoin in the treasure, Jon Collins-Black highlights its importance as a new frontier in the world of wealth. It serves as a reminder that treasure hunting today is not limited to digging through dirt or searching ancient ruins. It also involves understanding digital landscapes and navigating new technological terrain.

The Hunt for Bitcoin

Bitcoin's place in this treasure hunt offers a unique challenge. Unlike a tangible item, its presence might be signified by a hidden digital wallet or a private key stored in an unexpected location. To claim it, you'll need both physical exploration and intellectual savvy. Clues leading to Bitcoin will likely require knowledge of cryptography, finance, and the technological underpinnings of blockchain.

What Bitcoin Represents in This Journey

Bitcoin represents the future—not just of wealth but of treasure itself. Its inclusion underscores the idea that treasures are not static. They evolve, reflecting the changing priorities and values of society. In pursuing Bitcoin, you're not just hunting for a digital asset; you're embracing a new era of discovery, where treasure exists as much in the intangible as in the physical.

Antiques and Artifacts: Connecting to History

Among the treasures hidden in this remarkable hunt lies a collection of antiques and artifacts, each a window into a bygone era. These items are far more than objects; they are tangible pieces of history, holding the stories, triumphs, and tragedies of those who came before us. They bridge the past and present, reminding us that the lives and legacies of previous generations are woven into the fabric of our own.

This section of the treasure celebrates the power of artifacts to connect us with history, inviting you to not only uncover valuable items but also to immerse yourself in their significance.

The Significance of Antiques and Artifacts

Antiques and artifacts are more than relics; they are storytellers. Each one carries with it the echoes of its time, whether it is an 18th-century coin, a piece of ancient pottery, or a handwritten letter from a historic figure. These treasures are keys to understanding the cultures, values, and lives of those who lived in the past. They serve as reminders that history is not just a series of events but a collection of human experiences that shape who we are today.

What Treasures Await?

The antiques and artifacts included in this treasure hunt are as diverse as history itself. They have been carefully curated to represent a broad spectrum of time periods, cultures, and contexts. Here are a few examples of what you might discover:

1. **Artifacts of Everyday Life**:

- o Pottery, tools, or jewelry used by people centuries ago.

- o Items that tell stories of how ordinary individuals lived, worked, and thrived.

2. **Historical Significance**:

- o A pen used by a writer whose words changed the world.

- o A relic connected to a momentous event, such as a letter from the Civil War or a map used by explorers.

3. **Cultural Icons**:

- o Items crafted by master artisans, such as Louis Comfort Tiffany's stained glass or Pablo Picasso's sketches.

- o Pieces that represent pivotal artistic or cultural movements.

4. **Artifacts of Influence**:

- o Objects owned or used by figures like George Washington, Amelia Earhart, or Henry David Thoreau, offering a glimpse into their lives and contributions to history.

5. **Shipwreck Bounty**:

o Coins, jewels, or personal effects recovered from shipwrecks that hold untold tales of adventure and peril on the high seas.

Each item has been chosen not only for its monetary value but for the story it tells and the connection it offers to history.

The Hunt for Antiques and Artifacts

Finding these treasures requires more than luck. It calls for a curious mind and a respect for history. The clues leading to these items are deeply intertwined with the historical contexts in which they existed. To uncover them, you may need to:

- Research historical events, locations, and figures to decode clues.

- Delve into the craftsmanship and materials of specific periods to identify authentic artifacts.

- Explore locations of historical significance, such as abandoned settlements, old trading routes, or places tied to legendary events.

The process of seeking these treasures is itself a journey through time, as each step brings you closer to understanding the people and places that shaped the world.

Why Artifacts Matter Today

In a fast-paced world dominated by technology, antiques and artifacts remind us of the enduring importance of history. They ground us, offering a tangible link to the past and reminding us that we are part of a much larger story. By unearthing these items, you are preserving pieces of history that might otherwise be lost, ensuring that future generations can learn from and appreciate them.

The Value of Connecting to History

The treasures hidden in this hunt go beyond monetary worth. They hold intrinsic value as symbols of human resilience, creativity, and innovation. Owning a piece of history is not just a privilege but a responsibility—a chance to be a steward of the past. By participating in this treasure hunt, you're not only seeking artifacts; you're forging a deeper connection to the rich and diverse history of humanity.

Your Role as a Modern Explorer

As you embark on this journey, remember that you are not just a hunter of treasures; you are an explorer of stories. Each antique or artifact you find is an opportunity to step into the shoes of those who came before and to see the world as they saw it. The path you take will be as rewarding as the treasures you uncover, as every discovery will bring you closer to the heart of history.

Shipwreck Bounty: Sunken Riches

Beneath the waves of the world's oceans and seas lies a trove of forgotten treasures, the remains of countless shipwrecks that once carried dreams, wealth, and histories. These sunken riches have captured the imaginations of treasure hunters for centuries, their stories of peril, adventure, and loss waiting to be uncovered. The shipwreck bounty included in this treasure hunt is not just a collection of items; it's a portal to the maritime past, offering a glimpse into the lives and aspirations of those who sailed before us.

The Allure of Shipwreck Treasures

The romance of shipwrecks lies in their mystery and tragedy. Every ship that sank tells a tale: of voyages cut short, of storms that defied even the most skilled sailors, and of riches intended for distant shores that never reached their destinations. From merchant vessels laden with gold and silver to warships carrying artifacts of conquest and exploration, the treasures lost to the sea are as diverse as the oceans themselves.

But the allure goes beyond the material. Shipwrecks are time capsules, preserving items in conditions that can often be astonishingly pristine. Coins, jewelry, ceramics, weapons, and even mundane items like tools and navigational instruments can be found, offering insights into the culture, trade, and technology of their time.

What Treasures Await Beneath the Waves?

The shipwreck bounty included in this treasure hunt spans centuries and oceans, bringing together artifacts and riches that reflect the global nature of maritime exploration. Here's a glimpse of what may be part of the hunt:

1. **Gold and Silver Coins**:

   o Lost fortunes minted in the Americas, Europe, or Asia, representing a time when trade routes spanned the globe.

   o Coins bearing the insignia of monarchs or empires long past, each a testament to their influence.

2. **Jewelry and Precious Gems**:

   o Rings, necklaces, and brooches, often crafted with extraordinary skill, reflecting the tastes of an era.

- Loose gemstones like diamonds, emeralds, and sapphires that were destined for royalty or the wealthy elite.

3. **Ceramics and Porcelain**:

   - Items from renowned trade routes, such as fine china from Asia or earthenware from Europe.

   - Intricately painted vases and dishes that tell stories of craftsmanship and cultural exchange.

4. **Weapons and Artifacts of Warfare**:

   - Swords, cannons, and musket balls from naval battles, offering a glimpse into the military history of the seas.

   - Relics tied to historical conflicts, such as the Revolutionary War or pirate skirmishes.

5. **Personal Items**:

   - Letters, tools, and navigational equipment that humanize the tales of those who perished at sea.

   - Items that remind us of the sailors' hopes, fears, and the lives they left behind.

The Hunt for Shipwreck Bounty

Finding sunken treasures has always been one of the greatest challenges of treasure hunting. While modern technology has made the search more accessible, uncovering shipwreck artifacts still demands perseverance, skill, and a keen understanding of maritime history.

1. **Clues from the Past**:

   o The locations of these treasures may be tied to famous shipwrecks, historical trade routes, or stories of piracy and maritime warfare.

   o Old maps, journals, and historical accounts can help uncover the precise whereabouts of these underwater treasures.

2. **The Challenge of Recovery**:

   o While many shipwreck treasures lie beneath the sea, others may have been recovered and subsequently lost or hidden on land. You may need to search both the shores and the depths.

   o Clues in this treasure hunt will test your ability to connect history with geography, uncovering the stories behind the bounty.

3. **The Mystique of the Unknown**:

- Shipwreck treasures often come with unanswered questions: Who owned these items? Where were they headed? What caused the ship's demise? As you hunt for these riches, you're also piecing together a puzzle of history.

What Shipwreck Bounty Represents

Shipwreck treasures symbolize humanity's enduring relationship with the sea—a source of opportunity and danger, wealth and loss. These artifacts serve as reminders of the risks taken by explorers, merchants, and sailors who braved the open waters in search of trade, adventure, and survival.

The inclusion of shipwreck bounty in this treasure hunt also highlights the global interconnectedness of human history. Many of these items traveled across continents and oceans, reflecting the intricate web of trade and cultural exchange that defined past eras.

The Value Beyond Riches

While the monetary value of shipwreck artifacts can be immense, their true worth lies in the stories they tell. Each piece is a fragment of a larger narrative—a time when the world felt bigger, the seas more perilous, and exploration more daring. By uncovering these treasures, you're not just reclaiming wealth; you're preserving history, ensuring that the stories of these ships and their crews are not lost to the depths.

Your Role as a Modern-Day Explorer

As you pursue the shipwreck bounty in this treasure hunt, you are stepping into the role of a modern-day explorer. You will delve into the mysteries of the past, solving clues that bridge the gap between history and discovery. The items you uncover are not just treasures—they are keys to understanding the resilience, ambition, and ingenuity of humanity.

Whether your search leads you to sunken riches or simply to a deeper appreciation of the stories behind them, the journey will be one of adventure, learning, and connection to the enduring legacy of the sea.

In the treasure hunt for unimaginable riches, not all treasures are relics of ancient times or glimmers of gold. Some come from the modern era, born from pop culture, sports, and fandoms that have captivated millions. Rare collectibles—like Pokémon cards, sports memorabilia, and other unique items—add a contemporary flair to the treasure, making it a celebration of both nostalgia and the evolving definition of value.

These collectibles hold more than monetary worth; they represent cultural milestones, shared memories, and the passions of generations. Let's explore the excitement and significance behind these treasures and why they're an essential part of this ultimate hunt.

The Appeal of Rare Collectibles

Rare collectibles resonate because they evoke a sense of connection. Whether it's a Pokémon card you coveted as a child or a signed baseball from a legendary game, these items remind us of moments that transcended time— moments of awe, achievement, and pure joy. As tangible pieces of culture, they carry stories that link collectors and fans across decades.

But these items are not just sentimental; they are also sought-after investments. With markets for collectibles thriving worldwide, the value of rare Pokémon cards, sports memorabilia, and similar treasures has soared. Their combination of emotional and financial value makes them treasures in every sense of the word.

Treasures in This Hunt

The rare collectibles hidden in this treasure hunt are as diverse as the passions they represent. Here's a closer look at some of the remarkable finds that may await you:

1. Pokémon Cards: Nostalgia and Value

- **Iconic Cards**:

  - Highly coveted cards like the **First Edition Charizard (1999)** or the **Pikachu Illustrator Card**, known for their rarity and legendary status among fans.

  - Cards from limited-edition sets or special promotions, such as holographic cards and exclusive Japanese releases.

- **Why They Matter**:

  - Pokémon cards are more than trading cards; they are a cultural phenomenon. From the late 1990s to today, they have brought joy, strategy, and camaraderie to fans around the world.

  - These cards also represent a thriving collector's market, with certain cards fetching hundreds of thousands, even millions, of dollars at auctions.

2. Sports Memorabilia: The Legends of the Game

- **Historic Items**:

  - Signed baseballs, jerseys, or bats from iconic players like Babe Ruth, Jackie

Robinson, Michael Jordan, or Serena Williams.

- Items tied to unforgettable moments, such as a game-worn jersey from a championship game or a football used in a record-breaking play.

- **Why They Matter**:

  - Sports memorabilia preserves the legacy of athletes and their extraordinary achievements. These items embody the passion, talent, and determination that inspire fans worldwide.

  - They're also steeped in personal stories. For instance, a signed basketball from Michael Jordan might evoke memories of the 1996 NBA Finals—a pinnacle of sports history.

3. Other Unique Collectibles:

- **Pop Culture Icons**:

  - Limited-edition action figures, movie props, or comic books, like an original **Spider-Man #1** or a prop from a blockbuster film.

  - Rare toys, such as vintage Barbie dolls, Hot Wheels, or Star Wars figures from their earliest releases.

- **Trading Cards and Games**:

  - o Beyond Pokémon, other card games like Magic: The Gathering and Yu-Gi-Oh! have highly sought-after rarities.

  - o Rare board games or pieces from limited-edition game sets.

- **Limited-Edition Merchandise**:

  - o Items released in small quantities, such as watches, shoes, or branded collaborations from luxury and streetwear designers.

The Hunt for Rare Collectibles

Uncovering rare collectibles in this treasure hunt isn't just about chance—it's about understanding the stories and significance behind each item. The clues leading to these treasures will likely draw on themes of fandom, history, and culture. Here's what to expect:

1. **Decoding Clues**:

   - o The hunt may involve identifying locations tied to famous games, conventions, or moments in pop culture history.

- Clues might include references to iconic players, Pokémon lore, or even puzzles mimicking trading card challenges.

2. **Exploration**:

   - While some treasures may be hidden in obvious fan-favorite locations, others may be stashed in places connected to the origins of these collectibles.

   - For example, a Pokémon card might be hidden near a location tied to the franchise's creation, while sports memorabilia could be near a historic stadium.

3. **Community Knowledge**:

   - Fans of sports, Pokémon, or collectibles may hold the key to cracking the codes. Sharing knowledge and engaging with communities could be essential to success.

Why Rare Collectibles Matter

Rare collectibles reflect how deeply culture impacts our lives. They represent:

- **Nostalgia**: They bring back cherished memories of childhood, favorite games, or legendary sports moments.

- **Legacy**: Each item tells a story about the era and individuals it represents, preserving a cultural snapshot for future generations.

- **Connection**: Collectibles create shared experiences, bringing people together to celebrate their love for a team, a franchise, or a hobby.

The Value Beyond the Item

The true value of these collectibles isn't just in their rarity or monetary worth—it's in their ability to connect us to our passions. A signed baseball isn't just a piece of leather; it's a link to the grit and glory of an unforgettable game. A rare Pokémon card isn't just ink and cardboard; it's a reminder of battles fought and friendships forged in the world of Pokémon.

Your Role as a Collector of Stories

In this treasure hunt, your role is not just to find collectibles but to uncover and honor the stories they represent. Every item carries a piece of the past—a moment frozen in time that resonates with millions. By finding these treasures, you're preserving the passions and dreams of entire generations.

The Historical Treasures

Items from the Past: Treasures Owned by Legends

History is filled with extraordinary individuals who shaped the world through their courage, creativity, and vision. From explorers and inventors to artists and political leaders, these legends left behind not only their legacies but also the objects that accompanied their lives and work. These historical treasures are more than valuable artifacts—they are living connections to the stories of the past, holding the energy and significance of those who once owned them.

In this chapter, we delve into the world of historical treasures featured in this hunt: items that once belonged to legends and the secrets they carry.

The Significance of Historical Treasures

The allure of historical artifacts lies in their ability to transport us through time. When you hold an object once owned by a figure like George Washington, Amelia Earhart, or Pablo Picasso, you connect with their world. These treasures serve as tangible links to pivotal moments in history, allowing us to experience a slice of their lives and understand the context of their accomplishments.

Moreover, these items remind us that even the most legendary figures were human—people who used tools, carried mementos, and left behind artifacts that reflected their personalities, ambitions, and beliefs.

What Treasures Await?

The historical treasures in this hunt are as diverse as the legends who owned them. These artifacts have been chosen not only for their monetary value but for the cultural and emotional resonance they hold. Here are some of the treasures you might uncover:

1. Tools of Innovation

- A telescope or sextant used by a great explorer like Ferdinand Magellan or Sir Francis Drake, symbolic of humanity's drive to push boundaries and chart the unknown.

- An invention or prototype connected to visionaries like Thomas Edison or Nikola Tesla, offering a glimpse into the creative minds that changed the world.

2. Symbols of Leadership

- A handwritten letter or personal item from George Washington, Abraham Lincoln, or Theodore Roosevelt, representing their pivotal roles in shaping a nation.

- A ceremonial artifact, such as a sword or seal, once held by a monarch or leader during a critical period of history.

3. Artistic and Cultural Icons

- A paintbrush or palette used by Pablo Picasso, paired with sketches or notes revealing his creative process.

- A handwritten manuscript from a literary giant like Henry David Thoreau or Virginia Woolf, shedding light on the words and ideas that have inspired generations.

4. Aviation and Exploration

- Personal effects of Amelia Earhart, such as her flight goggles or a logbook, commemorating her groundbreaking journeys into the skies.

- A navigational chart or journal from an early expedition to uncharted territories, reminding us of the courage and curiosity of those who dared to explore.

5. Artifacts of Resilience

- An item carried by Jackie Onassis, symbolizing her grace and strength through history-shaping events.

- A relic from a survivor of a historical disaster, such as a lifeboat compass from the Titanic or a medal awarded for bravery in adversity.

The Hunt for Historical Treasures

Finding these treasures in this hunt will be as much about unraveling history as it is about locating hidden items. Here's how to navigate the clues and stories that lead to these iconic pieces:

1. **Research the Legends**:

   o Clues may require an understanding of the lives and timelines of these historical figures. Knowing key events, locations, and relationships in their lives will be essential to connecting the dots.

2. **Decode the Context**:

   o Clues will often hint at the cultural or political context of the time. For example, a reference to the signing of the Declaration of Independence might lead you to a treasure tied to a Founding Father.

3. **Explore Significant Locations**:

   o Treasures might be hidden in places of historical importance—such as the site of a famous speech, a groundbreaking invention, or an artistic milestone.

4. **Follow the Artifacts' Stories**:

   o Understanding the journey of an artifact, from its origin to its current location, can help you piece together the puzzle. Look for records of auctions, museum displays, or family heirlooms connected to the legends.

Why These Treasures Matter Today

In a world that often rushes forward, historical treasures remind us to pause and reflect. They teach us about resilience, creativity, and the power of individuals to shape the course of history. By seeking these treasures, you're not just collecting valuable items; you're preserving stories that inspire and educate future generations.

The Value of Ownership

Owning an artifact once touched by a legend is about more than its financial worth. It's about holding a piece of history in your hands—a connection to the people who challenged norms, inspired change, and left indelible marks on the world. These items carry the energy of their owners, offering a unique opportunity to feel closer to the past.

Your Role in Preserving History

As you uncover these treasures, you also become a guardian of their stories. Whether it's the pen used by Henry David Thoreau to write *Walden* or a relic tied to Amelia Earhart's daring flights, each item you discover is a chance to keep history alive. You're not just a treasure hunter; you're a storyteller, ensuring that the legacies of these figures endure for years to come.

Pablo Picasso is not just a name; it is an enduring symbol of creativity, genius, and the transformative power of art. As one of the most influential artists of the 20th century, Picasso revolutionized the art world with his daring innovation and limitless vision. From his pioneering role in the Cubist movement to his mastery of diverse styles and mediums, Picasso's works are celebrated as priceless cultural treasures. Yet, his legacy extends beyond the canvas, representing wealth in its many forms: artistic, intellectual, and material.

In this treasure hunt, objects connected to Picasso hold a unique allure. They are not merely artifacts of his life—

they are fragments of his brilliance, offering a window into the mind of a creative giant.

The Multifaceted Wealth of Picasso

Picasso's story is one of boundless wealth, but not just in the financial sense. His life and work encompass several dimensions of richness:

1. Artistic Wealth

- Picasso was a prolific artist who created over 50,000 works across his lifetime, including paintings, sculptures, ceramics, and prints.

- His groundbreaking innovations, particularly in Cubism, changed the way the world viewed art, dismantling traditional perspectives and reconstructing them in abstract, multifaceted ways.

- Works like *Les Demoiselles d'Avignon* and *Guernica* are considered masterpieces, blending technical brilliance with profound commentary on society, war, and human emotion.

2. Intellectual Wealth

- Picasso's genius lay in his ability to draw inspiration from diverse sources: classical art,

African masks, the Spanish Civil War, and personal relationships.

- His work reflected an ever-evolving exploration of identity, emotion, and the human condition, showcasing his intellectual curiosity and deep connection to global culture.

3. Financial Wealth

- Picasso's creations are among the most expensive artworks ever sold, with pieces like *Women of Algiers* fetching over $179 million at auction.

- During his lifetime, Picasso was a savvy businessman, ensuring his art was not only groundbreaking but also commercially successful.

- His name has become synonymous with artistic value, and items connected to him—from sketches to personal belongings—carry immense monetary and cultural worth.

Treasures Tied to Picasso in the Hunt

The treasures tied to Pablo Picasso in this hunt reflect the many facets of his legacy. Here's a glimpse of the items you might encounter:

1. Artistic Tools

- **Paintbrushes and Palettes**: Tools Picasso used to create his masterpieces, offering a direct connection to his process.

- **Sketches and Studies**: Preliminary drawings that reveal the evolution of his ideas, from concept to completion.

2. Finished Works and Fragments

- **Ceramics**: Picasso's exploration of pottery produced unique and collectible works that blend fine art with craftsmanship.

- **Prints**: Limited-edition lithographs and etchings, often signed by the artist, showcasing his versatility in different mediums.

3. Personal Artifacts

- **Letters and Notes**: Handwritten correspondence reflecting Picasso's thoughts on art, politics, and his personal relationships.

- **Objects Owned by Picasso**: Items such as a favorite piece of jewelry, a book from his library, or even a small trinket he cherished.

Why Picasso's Treasures Matter

The significance of Picasso's artifacts extends far beyond their monetary value:

1. **A Window into Creativity**

   o Picasso's tools and sketches reveal his thought process, offering a rare opportunity to see how a masterpiece takes shape.

   o They allow us to step into his studio and witness the spark of genius that transformed blank canvases into revolutionary art.

2. **A Reflection of History**

   o Picasso's life spanned a tumultuous era marked by wars, revolutions, and profound cultural shifts. His art often responded to these events, making his artifacts historical markers as well as personal relics.

3. **A Symbol of Enduring Influence**

   o Picasso's work continues to inspire artists, collectors, and historians worldwide. His treasures remind us of the timeless power of creativity to reshape our understanding of the world.

The Hunt for Picasso's Legacy

Finding treasures connected to Picasso will require not only a knowledge of his art but also an understanding of his life. Here are some tips for uncovering thcsc priceless artifacts:

1. **Study His Life**

   o Learn about Picasso's major periods, such as his Blue Period, Rose Period, and Cubist innovations, to interpret clues related to his artistic journey.

   o Familiarize yourself with key locations in his life, like his birthplace in Málaga, Spain, his studios in Paris, and his final home in Mougins, France.

2. **Understand the Symbolism**

   o Picasso often used recurring symbols in his work, such as doves, bulls, and harlequins. These motifs might appear in the clues leading to his treasures.

3. **Follow the Legacy**

   o Many of Picasso's artifacts are tied to famous auctions, museums, or exhibitions. Tracing their history could provide vital hints.

Picasso's Legacy: A Wealth Beyond Measure

Pablo Picasso's name is synonymous with the transformative power of art. His treasures represent more than personal or financial wealth—they embody a legacy of innovation, passion, and cultural significance. To uncover an artifact connected to Picasso is to claim a piece of this legacy, a fragment of the brilliance that continues to shape the art world.

Your Role in Honoring Picasso's Genius

As you search for treasures tied to Picasso, remember that you're not just uncovering items—you're preserving the spirit of an artist who dared to see the world differently. His art challenges us to embrace creativity, question norms, and find beauty in the unexpected.

By finding and safeguarding his treasures, you become part of Picasso's story, ensuring that his legacy continues to inspire future generations.

Are you ready to step into the world of Picasso and uncover the treasures that reflect his unmatched genius? The art of wealth awaits.

Andrew Carnegie: American Industrial Riches

Andrew Carnegie's name is synonymous with the transformative power of ambition, innovation, and philanthropy. Rising from humble beginnings as a Scottish immigrant to the United States, he became one of the wealthiest individuals in history, revolutionizing the steel industry and redefining what it meant to achieve the American Dream. Carnegie's legacy is not just one of industrial wealth but also one of intellectual, cultural, and philanthropic riches, leaving an indelible mark on American society and the world.

Treasures connected to Andrew Carnegie in this hunt are more than artifacts—they are symbols of industry, ingenuity, and the enduring impact of generosity.

The Rise of Andrew Carnegie: From Rags to Riches

Carnegie's journey is a quintessential tale of upward mobility, hard work, and visionary thinking:

- **Early Struggles**: Born in 1835 in Dunfermline, Scotland, Carnegie immigrated to the United States at age 13. He started his career as a bobbin boy in a textile factory and later worked as a telegraph operator.

- **Breaking Into Business**: Carnegie's talent for innovation and efficiency shone when he entered the railroad industry. He rapidly advanced, leveraging his positions to gain valuable insights into transportation and infrastructure.

- **The Steel Revolution**: In the 1870s, Carnegie invested in steel production, introducing groundbreaking methods that dramatically increased efficiency and lowered costs. His company, Carnegie Steel, became the largest and most profitable industrial enterprise of its time.

- **A Legacy of Wealth**: By 1901, Carnegie sold his steel empire to J.P. Morgan for $480 million (equivalent to over $15 billion today), cementing his place among the wealthiest individuals in history.

The Wealth of Carnegie's Influence

Carnegie's riches extended far beyond financial wealth. He embodied a multidimensional legacy that continues to inspire:

1. Industrial Wealth

Carnegie's innovations in steel production powered the growth of modern infrastructure. Bridges, railroads, and skyscrapers owe their existence to the affordability and accessibility of Carnegie Steel.

2. Intellectual Wealth

Carnegie was a firm believer in the power of knowledge and self-improvement. He authored books like *The Gospel of Wealth*, which articulated his philosophy of using wealth for the greater good, inspiring future generations of philanthropists.

3. Cultural and Social Wealth

Carnegie's generosity transformed communities. He funded the creation of over 2,500 public libraries worldwide, donated to universities, and supported scientific research, arts, and global peace initiatives.

Treasures Tied to Carnegie in the Hunt

The treasures connected to Andrew Carnegie reflect his life, achievements, and enduring values. These artifacts symbolize not just material wealth but also the principles he championed:

1. Industrial Memorabilia

- **Tools and Equipment**: A rivet or steel ingot produced in Carnegie's mills, representing the backbone of American industrialization.

- **Blueprints and Documents**: Original plans for a steel plant or contracts signed by Carnegie, offering a glimpse into his empire-building strategies.

2. Personal Belongings

- **Carnegie's Writing Desk**: The very place where he penned *The Gospel of Wealth*, encouraging the ethical use of riches.

- **Handwritten Letters**: Personal correspondence revealing his thoughts on business, philanthropy, and world peace.

3. Philanthropic Artifacts

- **Library Dedication Plaques**: Original markers from one of his libraries, commemorating his commitment to education.

- **Peace Medals and Awards**: Honors Carnegie received for his efforts to promote international harmony.

4. Historical Items

- **Carnegie Steel Bonds or Stock Certificates**: Financial relics representing the empire that redefined global industry.

- **Artifacts from Carnegie Hall**: Objects from the iconic music venue he funded, showcasing his love for the arts.

Why Carnegie's Legacy Matters Today

Carnegie's life story and philosophy remain profoundly relevant:

1. **The Power of Vision**: Carnegie demonstrated how strategic thinking, innovation, and hard work can transform industries and create lasting change.

2. **The Importance of Giving Back**: His philanthropic philosophy teaches that wealth is a responsibility, not just a privilege. His belief that "a man who dies rich dies disgraced" continues to inspire modern philanthropists like Bill Gates and Warren Buffett.

3. **The Role of Infrastructure**: Carnegie's investments in steel were crucial in building the backbone of modern America, from its cities to its transportation networks.

The Hunt for Carnegie's Treasures

Uncovering treasures tied to Andrew Carnegie requires an understanding of his life, his industry, and his philanthropy. Here's how to approach the search:

1. **Explore His Industrial Footprint**

    o Study the locations of his steel mills, railroads, and industrial hubs, as treasures may be hidden in areas significant to his business empire.

2. **Follow His Philanthropic Trail**

   o Focus on the libraries, universities, and cultural institutions he founded. Clues may point to these landmarks, which remain testaments to his generosity.

3. **Decode His Philosophy**

   o Clues referencing *The Gospel of Wealth* or his advocacy for world peace could lead you to treasures reflecting his values and beliefs.

Carnegie's Wealth in Perspective

Andrew Carnegie's riches were more than a measure of his financial success—they were tools he used to shape society. His life is a reminder that wealth is not just about accumulation but about its transformative potential. The treasures tied to him are not merely relics of the past; they are beacons of a philosophy that urges us to strive for personal success while uplifting others.

Your Role in Preserving Carnegie's Legacy

As you uncover treasures connected to Carnegie, you step into the shoes of an industrial titan and a visionary philanthropist. Each artifact you find is an opportunity to honor the principles he stood for: innovation, perseverance, and the ethical stewardship of wealth.

Are you ready to connect with the riches of Andrew Carnegie and carry forward his legacy of progress and generosity? The treasures of industry and philanthropy await.

George Washington: The Legacy of a Nation

George Washington is far more than a historical figure; he is the very embodiment of American ideals. As the first President of the United States, Commander-in-Chief of the Continental Army during the Revolutionary War, and a key architect of the nation's founding principles, Washington's legacy defines patriotism, leadership, and vision.

Treasures tied to Washington in this hunt are not merely relics of his life—they are symbols of the values he championed: freedom, unity, and the pursuit of a better future. They connect us to the birth of the United States and offer a glimpse into the life of the man often called the "Father of His Country."

Washington's Life: A Legacy of Service and Sacrifice

1. The Early Years

Born on February 22, 1732, in Westmoreland County, Virginia, George Washington grew up on a plantation and honed his skills as a surveyor and landowner. His early experiences with the frontier taught him the value of hard work and resilience.

2. Revolutionary Leadership

Washington's defining moment came during the American Revolution. Appointed as Commander-in-Chief of the Continental Army, he led a ragtag group of soldiers against the formidable British forces. Despite overwhelming odds, his strategic brilliance and unwavering resolve secured victory and independence for the United States.

3. The First President

Unanimously elected as the first President of the United States in 1789, Washington set the standard for leadership, voluntarily stepping down after two terms to establish a precedent of peaceful transitions of power. His Farewell Address remains a guiding document for American politics.

4. Farmer and Statesman

After retiring from public office, Washington returned to his beloved Mount Vernon plantation, where he demonstrated a commitment to agricultural innovation and sustainable farming practices.

The Multifaceted Legacy of George Washington

Washington's contributions to the United States are unparalleled, leaving behind a legacy of values and accomplishments that continue to inspire:

1. The Revolutionary Leader

- Washington's leadership during the Revolutionary War defined his character. His ability to rally diverse groups toward a common cause exemplified his commitment to unity and perseverance.

2. The Visionary Statesman

- As president, Washington laid the foundation for the U.S. government, overseeing the establishment of the Constitution, the Bill of Rights, and the first Cabinet. His decisions shaped the executive branch and the country's future.

3. The Symbol of Unity

- Washington's refusal to align with political parties underscored his belief in national unity above partisanship. His dedication to the idea of one united nation remains a powerful symbol.

Treasures Tied to Washington in the Hunt

Artifacts connected to George Washington represent his leadership, personal life, and the founding of the United States. Each treasure carries a story of resilience, innovation, and hope:

1. Revolutionary Relics

- **Personal Weapons**: Items such as Washington's sword or pistols, used during the Revolutionary War, symbolize his courage and military prowess.

- **Battlefield Maps**: Hand-drawn maps of key battles, showcasing his strategic mind and command of the war effort.

2. Presidential Artifacts

- **Letters and Speeches**: Handwritten documents, including drafts of his Farewell Address, reveal his thoughts on governance and the future of the nation.

- **Presidential Seal**: Early designs of the seal of the United States, associated with Washington's administration.

3. Personal Belongings

- **Mount Vernon Memorabilia**: Farming tools, furniture, or even pieces of his estate reflect his life as a planter and innovator.

- **Clothing and Accessories**: Items like Washington's tricorne hat or boots offer an intimate connection to his daily life.

4. Foundational Documents

- **Constitutional Artifacts**: Items tied to the Constitutional Convention, where Washington presided, serve as reminders of his role in shaping American democracy.

The Symbolism of Washington's Treasures

The treasures tied to George Washington are more than historical artifacts—they represent ideals that continue to define the United States:

1. **Courage and Leadership**

   - Washington's personal effects from the Revolutionary War capture the bravery and determination that secured American independence.

2. **Unity and Vision**

   - His presidential relics remind us of his commitment to creating a united and enduring nation, even in its infancy.

3. **Resilience and Innovation**

o Items from Mount Vernon reflect Washington's forward-thinking approach to agriculture and his desire to build a self-sufficient and prosperous country.

Hunting for Washington's Legacy

Finding treasures tied to George Washington requires an understanding of his life, values, and the pivotal moments of his era. Here's how to approach the search:

1. **Explore Revolutionary Sites**

   o Study key locations like Valley Forge, Yorktown, and Boston, where Washington's presence shaped history.

2. **Follow His Presidency**

   o Look for clues tied to New York and Philadelphia, the early capitals of the United States, and sites significant to his administration.

3. **Learn About Mount Vernon**

   o Washington's estate remains a treasure trove of historical significance. Items tied to this location could hold the key to unlocking clues.

Why Washington's Legacy Endures

George Washington's life and accomplishments continue to resonate because they embody timeless principles:

- **Service Before Self**: His dedication to the Revolution and the presidency showed a willingness to sacrifice personal gain for the good of the nation.

- **Integrity in Leadership**: Washington's commitment to fairness and unity set a standard for future leaders.

- **A Vision of Freedom**: His belief in liberty and justice provided the foundation for the American experiment in democracy.

Your Role in Preserving Washington's Legacy

As you search for treasures tied to George Washington, remember that you're not just uncovering objects—you're connecting with the roots of a nation. Each artifact is a piece of a larger story about resilience, courage, and the enduring quest for freedom.

By honoring his legacy, you become a part of his vision, ensuring that the ideals he championed continue to inspire future generations.

Are you ready to embark on a journey into the past and uncover the treasures of the man who shaped a nation? The legacy of George Washington awaits.

Amelia Earhart: The Spirit of Adventure

Amelia Earhart's name is forever etched in history as a daring aviator, a trailblazer for women's rights, and a symbol of boundless curiosity. Her fearless attitude and groundbreaking achievements in aviation made her an icon of exploration and perseverance. Earhart's disappearance during her attempt to circumnavigate the globe in 1937 only heightened her mystique, cementing her legacy as one of history's most enduring adventurers.

Treasures tied to Earhart evoke her unyielding spirit and her commitment to pushing the boundaries of possibility.

The Sky Is No Limit: Amelia Earhart's Journey

1. **Early   Life   and   Aspirations**
   Born in 1897 in Atchison, Kansas, Earhart was fascinated by adventure from an early age. Inspired by a stunt-flying exhibition in 1920, she took her first flight and was hooked, vowing to make aviation her life's work.

2. **Trailblazing Achievements**

- In 1928, she became the first woman to fly across the Atlantic Ocean as a passenger, earning international acclaim.

- In 1932, she flew solo across the Atlantic, becoming the first woman—and second person after Charles Lindbergh—to accomplish the feat.

- Earhart also set altitude records and worked to open doors for women in aviation, proving that no field was out of reach.

3. **The Final Flight**

Her attempt to fly around the globe ended in mystery when her plane disappeared over the Pacific Ocean. This unsolved enigma adds a layer of intrigue to her legacy.

Treasures Tied to Earhart in the Hunt

Artifacts related to Amelia Earhart are symbols of her courage and relentless pursuit of dreams:

- **Flight Logs**: Original entries from her historic solo Atlantic crossing.

- **Pilot Gear**: Items like her iconic leather jacket, goggles, or flight maps.

- **Correspondence**: Letters detailing her thoughts on aviation, women's rights, and exploration.

Jackie Onassis: A Life of Elegance

Jacqueline Kennedy Onassis was more than a First Lady; she was an icon of grace, intelligence, and resilience. Her influence extended far beyond her role as the wife of President John F. Kennedy, as she became a cultural and fashion symbol, a patron of the arts, and a woman of remarkable inner strength.

Treasures tied to Jackie Onassis reflect her sophistication, her love for culture, and her profound impact on American history.

The Many Facets of Jackie's Life

1. The Iconic First Lady

- Jackie transformed the role of First Lady, bringing a sense of elegance and cultural refinement to the White House.

- She spearheaded the restoration of the White House, preserving its historical significance and making it a symbol of American pride.

2. The Fashion Muse

- Jackie's impeccable style—marked by pillbox hats, tailored suits, and timeless accessories—made her a global fashion icon.

- Her understated elegance continues to influence fashion and design.

3. **The Woman of Strength**

- After JFK's assassination, Jackie became a symbol of dignity and strength, guiding her family and the nation through tragedy.

- Later in life, she built a successful career in publishing and maintained her private life with grace and composure.

Treasures Tied to Jackie Onassis in the Hunt

Treasures connected to Jackie are a testament to her taste, intellect, and legacy:

- **Fashion Pieces**: A pillbox hat, pearl necklace, or gloves that reflect her iconic style.

- **White House Restoration Documents**: Blueprints, letters, or artifacts from her historic project.

- **Personal Correspondence**: Letters revealing her thoughts on art, culture, and her vision for the nation.

Henry David Thoreau: The Wisdom of Simplicity

Henry David Thoreau, the 19th-century transcendentalist, naturalist, and philosopher, is best known for his writings on simple living, self-reliance, and the interconnectedness of humanity and nature. His work continues to inspire those seeking clarity and purpose in a world dominated by materialism.

Treasures tied to Thoreau reflect his philosophy of simplicity and his deep connection to the natural world.

Thoreau's Life: A Journey Toward Simplicity

1. **Life   at   Walden   Pond**
   In 1845, Thoreau famously retreated to a cabin he built near Walden Pond in Concord, Massachusetts, where he lived for two years, chronicling his reflections on nature, society, and self-reliance. These musings became the foundation for his seminal work, *Walden*.

2. **Advocate   for   Civil   Liberties**
   Thoreau's essay *Civil Disobedience* argued for

individual moral responsibility in the face of unjust laws, influencing figures like Gandhi and Martin Luther King Jr.

3. **Nature as Teacher**
Thoreau believed in learning from the natural world and saw nature as a source of spiritual insight, creativity, and fulfillment.

Treasures Tied to Thoreau in the Hunt

Items associated with Thoreau serve as reminders of the beauty of simplicity and the power of individual thought:

- **Original Manuscripts**: Drafts or pages from *Walden* or *Civil Disobedience*.

- **Personal Items**: A quill pen, journal, or a replica of his handmade tools from Walden Pond.

- **Nature Artifacts**: Pressed flowers, sketches, or maps he used during his explorations.

The Enduring Impact of These Figures

Each of these individuals—Amelia Earhart, Jackie Onassis, and Henry David Thoreau—represents a unique aspect of human potential: the courage to explore, the grace to lead, and the wisdom to reflect. Treasures tied to their lives are not just relics of the past; they are gateways to understanding their spirit and continuing their legacies.

Through this treasure hunt, you have the opportunity to connect with their stories and embody the values they represent: adventure, elegance, and simplicity.

Louis Comfort Tiffany: Art Nouveau Treasures

Louis Comfort Tiffany, a master of Art Nouveau design, revolutionized the decorative arts by blending nature-inspired themes with innovative craftsmanship. Known for his exquisite stained glass works, jewelry, and mosaics, Tiffany's creations are synonymous with elegance, creativity, and timeless beauty.

As a pioneer of Art Nouveau in America, Tiffany's designs transformed the way people viewed functional objects, elevating lamps, windows, and vases into works of art. Treasures tied to Tiffany capture the essence of this artistic movement, characterized by organic forms, vibrant colors, and intricate detail.

The Life and Legacy of Louis Comfort Tiffany

1. **Early Life and Influences**

   o Born in 1848, Tiffany was the son of Charles Lewis Tiffany, founder of the famous Tiffany & Co. jewelry brand.

Though he initially pursued painting, Tiffany eventually shifted to decorative arts, where his innovative techniques found their greatest expression.

2. **Innovations in Stained Glass**

   o Tiffany developed a revolutionary technique known as "favrile glass," which involved embedding metallic oxides into the glass, producing iridescent hues that changed with light.

   o His iconic stained glass windows and lamps often depicted nature—flowers, trees, and peacocks—bringing vibrant life into functional art.

3. **Art Nouveau Movement**

   o As a leader in the Art Nouveau style, Tiffany's work reflected its emphasis on flowing, organic forms inspired by nature. His designs broke away from traditional rigid structures, celebrating curves, asymmetry, and bold experimentation.

4. **Enduring Impact**

   o Tiffany's contributions to design extended beyond his art objects to include interiors of churches, public buildings, and private homes. His work remains a testament to the marriage of utility and beauty.

Treasures Tied to Louis Comfort Tiffany

Items connected to Tiffany represent the pinnacle of craftsmanship and artistic vision:

- **Stained Glass Windows**: Miniature replicas or fragments of original Tiffany windows, featuring intricate floral or abstract designs.

- **Tiffany Lamps**: Authentic or reproduction bases and shades that showcase his distinctive use of color and form.

- **Jewelry and Vases**: Pieces crafted with favrile glass or precious metals, embodying the spirit of Art Nouveau.

- **Sketches and Patterns**: Original designs or blueprints used in Tiffany's workshops.

The Forrest Fenn Treasure: A Legacy of Hidden Riches

The Forrest Fenn Treasure captivated the imagination of thousands, inspiring a modern-day treasure hunt that spanned over a decade. Hidden in the Rocky Mountains by art dealer and author Forrest Fenn, the chest contained an array of gold, jewels, and historical artifacts, valued at over $1 million.

Fenn's treasure was more than just a collection of riches—it was a call to adventure, a puzzle to solve, and a reminder of the thrill of discovery. The hunt for this elusive prize forged a legacy that continues to inspire treasure hunters worldwide.

The Story Behind the Treasure

1. **Forrest Fenn's Vision**

   o In 2010, Forrest Fenn announced that he had buried a chest filled with treasures somewhere in the Rocky Mountains. He aimed to inspire people to explore nature and find adventure.

2. **The Clues**

   o Fenn published a poem in his memoir *The Thrill of the Chase*, which contained cryptic clues leading to the treasure's location. The poem's riddles were open to interpretation, sparking debate and analysis among hunters.

3. **The Discovery**

o   After nearly 10 years, the treasure was found in 2020 by an anonymous hunter. Its exact location and many details remain a mystery, adding to its legendary status.

4. **The Treasure's Contents**

o   The chest included gold coins, nuggets, pre-Columbian artifacts, jade carvings, and an assortment of other rare and valuable items.

The Legacy of the Forrest Fenn Treasure

The hunt for Fenn's treasure left an indelible mark on the world of exploration and adventure:

1. **The Joy of Discovery**

o   Fenn's treasure rekindled a sense of wonder and curiosity, encouraging people to embrace the unknown.

2. **A Puzzle for All**

o   The clues in *The Thrill of the Chase* challenged hunters to think critically, research meticulously, and work collaboratively.

3. **Connection to Nature**

- By situating the treasure in the Rocky Mountains, Fenn inspired participants to explore the wilderness and appreciate its beauty.

Treasures Tied to the Forrest Fenn Legacy

Artifacts linked to the Fenn treasure hunt symbolize the enduring appeal of mystery and exploration:

- **Replica Gold Nuggets and Coins**: Representing the literal wealth hidden in the chest.

- **A Copy of *The Thrill of the Chase***: Annotated with Fenn's original poem and key insights into the hunt.

- **Map of the Rocky Mountains**: Highlighting regions explored during the decade-long search.

- **Artifacts from the Treasure**: Reproductions of items like the jade carvings or ceremonial masks found in the chest.

Exploring the Spirit of Adventure and Art

Both Louis Comfort Tiffany and Forrest Fenn left behind legacies rooted in creativity and exploration. Tiffany's treasures invite us to see the world's beauty through an artist's lens, while Fenn's hunt reminds us of the thrill of the unknown and the joy of discovery.

Together, their contributions remind us that treasures—whether crafted by human hands or buried beneath the earth—hold the power to connect us to the past, inspire the present, and ignite dreams for the future. Will you be the one to uncover their secrets? The journey awaits.

The Treasure Hunt: How to Begin

Embarking on a treasure hunt is no ordinary adventure—it's a journey that calls for curiosity, creativity, and, most of all, determination. Whether you're searching for a hidden fortune like the Forrest Fenn treasure or seeking to uncover priceless artifacts tied to history and legend, the thrill of the chase is what makes the treasure hunt a transformative experience. But how do you start? How do you decode the map, follow the clues, and ultimately find the treasure?

In this chapter, we will break down the essential steps to begin your treasure-hunting journey, from deciphering cryptic clues to getting your hands on the right tools and setting out into the unknown.

Decoding the Map: The Hunt Begins

The treasure map is your first key to unlocking the mystery of the hidden riches. Whether it's an actual physical map or a collection of cryptic clues written in poems, riddles, or ancient texts, decoding it is where the adventure truly begins. Every map has its own language and system, and understanding its intricacies is the first step in your quest.

Step 1: Understanding the Map and Clues

1. **Literal vs. Figurative Clues**

   o   In treasure hunts, clues can come in both literal and figurative forms. Literal clues might be places on a map, landmarks, or specific objects, while figurative clues require interpretation—be it a poem, an object's symbolism, or even geographical hints hidden in the words.

   o   For example, Forrest Fenn's treasure was hidden with the help of a poem that contained geographical and metaphorical clues. Decoding these meant not just knowing how to read a map, but also how to understand the deeper layers of meaning.

2. **Look for Repetition or Patterns**

   o   Treasure maps often hide their secrets through repetition. Pay attention to words, locations, or phrases that appear multiple times—these may be significant markers or may point you toward areas of focus. In some cases, repetition could indicate a pattern to follow on the ground or in the terrain.

- o If you're working with a map that has a symbolic language, like those found in ancient treasure hunts, recurring motifs often suggest hidden meanings.

3. **Understanding Geographic Features**

- o Topography is critical in most treasure hunts. Mountains, rivers, valleys, or even distinct trees or rock formations often feature in treasure maps. The way these geographical features are represented may differ, so it's crucial to familiarize yourself with the terrain in the area of the hunt.

- o Use modern maps or digital tools to help cross-reference the features in the treasure map. Sometimes, historical maps may provide additional context that could unlock certain paths or clues.

Step 2: Preparing Your Gear and Resources

With your map in hand, you need the right tools to begin your treasure hunt. Here are the essentials for a successful adventure:

1. **Proper Gear**

o **Topographical Maps**: In addition to the treasure map, you'll need detailed, accurate topographical maps that show the lay of the land. These maps often mark elevation, water sources, and natural landmarks— critical elements in identifying the treasure's location.

o **Compass and GPS**: A compass will help orient you when you venture into the wild, while a GPS device is essential for pinpointing exact coordinates. In many treasure hunts, coordinates are crucial for precise navigation, especially in remote or dense areas.

o **Notebooks and Journals**: Always carry a journal to document your observations and interpretations. Treasure hunts often involve trial and error, and having a record of your ideas, hunches, and findings will guide you toward the next clue.

2. **Safety and Survival Tools**

o Always be prepared for the unknown. Depending on the terrain, your hunt might lead you through forests, mountains, deserts, or even oceans. Equip yourself with essential survival tools such as a first-aid kit, sturdy hiking boots, weather-appropriate clothing, and a flashlight.

- o A small survival kit with a multi-tool, emergency whistle, and matches can be life-saving in extreme conditions. The treasure hunt could take you to places far from civilization, so preparedness is key.

3. **Research and Historical Context**

- o **Historical Research**: Knowledge is power when it comes to treasure hunting. Conduct in-depth research about the history surrounding the treasure. Who hid it, why, and what was the context in which it was placed? Sometimes the story of the treasure itself can offer important clues.

- o Look into the history of places tied to the treasure, particularly if it's linked to an ancient civilization or famous person. Understanding the historical significance of the site and its inhabitants could help you decipher symbolic language or understand what types of materials you might be seeking.

Step 3: Analyzing the Environment

Once you're on the ground, it's time to analyze your surroundings carefully. A map is only as good as the way you interpret the land in front of you.

1. **Read the Terrain**

   o Walk the land with purpose, and use your map and compass to confirm landmarks or terrain features. Look for the natural objects, formations, or patterns mentioned in your clues. The treasure might not be immediately visible; instead, the path to it could involve carefully studying the environment and piecing together small clues.

   o Always be patient and methodical. Keep in mind that treasure hunts require focus and persistence. Trust your instincts, but don't rush. Sometimes, treasure lies just below the surface, in a spot that seems inconspicuous.

2. **Interpreting Natural Signs**

   o Pay attention to animal tracks, plant growth, rock formations, and water paths. These can sometimes indicate hidden paths or suggest areas where the treasure might be buried or stashed. In some hunts, legends claim that the treasure is hidden under certain types of trees, beneath unusual rocks, or near a specific water source.

- o If you're searching in an area known for treasure hunts, such as the Rocky Mountains or a forest linked to ancient tribes, study the local ecosystem. Some clues might be related to seasonal patterns or specific plant life.

Step 4: Collaborating and Problem-Solving

Treasure hunting is rarely a solitary pursuit. Collaborating with other hunters or consulting experts can help you tackle difficult clues or ideas you might not have considered.

1. **Forming a Team**

   - o Depending on the complexity of the hunt, forming a team can increase your chances of success. Teams bring diverse skills to the table—mapping, navigation, historical knowledge, problem-solving, and physical endurance. Working with others allows you to discuss ideas, challenge each other's assumptions, and combine your findings.

   - o However, teamwork requires effective communication. Share findings and theories without jumping to conclusions, and keep track of what each person uncovers to avoid repeating work or overlooking clues.

2. Consulting Experts

- o If you find yourself stumped by a particular clue or unable to understand a symbol, don't hesitate to consult experts. Historians, archaeologists, cryptographers, and even local guides can offer insights that might unlock the puzzle. Sometimes, a professional's perspective can reveal something you missed.

Step 5: Keep Your Wits About You

No matter how much preparation you put in, remember that a treasure hunt is a journey of discovery—and not always of riches. The real treasure is often in the process of solving the puzzle, connecting the dots, and understanding the history behind the hunt. Stay persistent, keep learning, and savor every moment of the adventure.

Clues, Riddles, and Challenges: How to Solve Them

Treasure hunting is as much about the thrill of the chase as it is about the art of problem-solving. In this world of hidden treasures, clues, riddles, and challenges are your roadmaps, leading you from one discovery to the next. Whether it's an ancient puzzle, a cryptic message, or a riddle wrapped in a mystery, the process of solving these challenges is what makes the hunt so exhilarating. But how do you approach solving clues and riddles that may seem impossible to decipher at first glance? This chapter delves into effective strategies for cracking the codes, unraveling the mysteries, and navigating the challenges that stand between you and the treasure.

Step 1: Understanding the Nature of the Clue

The first step in solving any clue is understanding its nature. Clues come in many forms—literal, figurative, visual, or auditory. It's important to know what type of clue you're dealing with so you can approach it with the right mindset.

Types of Clues

1. **Literal Clues**
   These are straightforward and direct pieces of
   information. They might be geographical markers,
   such as "near the old oak tree," or they could be
   more specific, like coordinates or the name of a
   place. Literal clues are often the easiest to decode
   because they tell you exactly what you need to
   know. However, they can also be tricky if they're
   hidden in plain sight or involve historical or
   symbolic significance.

2. **Figurative Clues**
   Figurative clues require interpretation and creative
   thinking. These could come in the form of
   metaphors, riddles, or symbolic references. A clue
   like "where the eagle soars" might refer to a place
   with a connection to eagles—like a mountain range
   where they are often spotted—or it could hint at a
   location associated with something symbolic, such
   as a city or landmark named after the bird.
   Understanding the symbolism and metaphor behind
   these clues is essential.

3. **Visual Clues**
   Sometimes, the treasure map or the surroundings
   you're exploring will offer visual clues. These could
   include patterns, colors, or unusual marks on a map
   or in the environment. Visual clues might be harder

to decipher because they often rely on perception, but they can be incredibly rewarding when cracked.

4. **Auditory and Olfactory Clues**
   On rare occasions, treasure hunts may include clues based on sound or smell. For instance, a clue might involve listening for the sound of running water or identifying a particular scent in a cave. These sensory clues can require heightened awareness and patience but offer an immersive experience.

Step 2: Breaking Down Riddles

Riddles are among the most popular—and challenging—types of clues in a treasure hunt. They force you to think outside the box and require not only logic but also imagination. But how do you crack a riddle that doesn't make sense at first?

Strategies for Solving Riddles

1. **Look for Wordplay**
   Riddles often rely on puns, wordplay, and multiple meanings of words. Pay attention to the possible double meanings of words in the riddle. For example, if the riddle mentions "the brightest star in the sky," it might refer to the literal star, or it could point to a famous landmark named after a star.

Consider the many meanings a single word might have.

2. **Break the Riddle into Parts**

   A riddle is often made up of multiple components. Rather than trying to solve it all at once, break it down into manageable sections. Identify the subject of the riddle, any clues about location, time, or objects, and then try to understand how these pieces fit together. You may uncover the solution more easily when you tackle each element individually.

3. **Use Lateral Thinking**

   Lateral thinking is a technique where you approach problems from unexpected angles. Rather than thinking about the riddle in a linear, logical fashion, try to see if the answer could be something unconventional or surprising. For instance, if the riddle talks about a "mysterious island," don't immediately jump to the assumption that it refers to an actual landmass. The "island" might be metaphorical—like an isolated spot in the wilderness or a remote location on a map.

4. **Identify Patterns or Rhythms**

   Many riddles use rhyme or rhythm to convey their clues. If the riddle is written in verse, pay attention to the cadence and rhyme scheme—it might be trying to direct your attention to specific letters or words. For example, certain lines might give you

the first letter of each word in a hidden phrase or
acronym.

5. **Consult References or Resources**
   If you're stuck, don't be afraid to consult outside
   resources. Many riddles are based on historical,
   literary, or cultural references. Familiarity with
   mythology, literature, or even the local history of
   the treasure site can provide valuable insights into
   solving riddles that might otherwise seem
   inscrutable.

Step 3: Solving Visual Clues

Visual clues are often the most difficult to solve because
they require you to see beyond the obvious. Whether
they're encoded images, obscure landmarks, or hidden
symbols, these clues need keen observation and sometimes
a fresh perspective.

Strategies for Interpreting Visual Clues

1. **Focus on the Details**
   The smallest details in a map or visual clue might
   hold the key to unraveling the mystery. Pay close
   attention to unusual features like shapes, angles, or
   color contrasts. If you're dealing with a map, for
   example, an obscure mark might be hiding a hidden
   location or an important landmark.

2. **Look for Hidden Patterns**
   Visual clues often work through symmetry or pattern recognition. For example, an image might contain a repeated symbol, or the shape of an object might align with the outlines of a well-known landmark. Explore the possibility that the visual clue is guiding you toward a hidden path or location.

3. **Use Modern Technology**
   Sometimes the visual clues you encounter are too complex or obscure to decipher with the naked eye. Don't hesitate to use technology to enhance your vision. Digital imaging software or photo-editing tools can reveal hidden layers in photographs, maps, or documents, such as watermarks, faint lines, or patterns that are invisible to the naked eye.

4. **Consult with Experts**
   If you're dealing with art, historical landmarks, or specific cultural symbols, seeking advice from experts in the field can be invaluable. Archaeologists, art historians, and local experts may help you identify important details that otherwise would be overlooked.

Step 4: Overcoming Mental and Physical Challenges

Treasure hunting doesn't just test your mind—it challenges your body and your resilience. Navigating harsh terrains, deciphering difficult clues, and staying motivated over long periods can be taxing.

How to Stay Focused and Resilient

1. **Persevere Through Frustration**
   There will be times when the clues don't seem to add up, when progress feels slow, or when the treasure feels out of reach. Remember that persistence is key. Take breaks, re-assess the clues, and approach the challenge with renewed energy. Sometimes stepping away for a while can give you fresh insight.

2. **Manage Your Time**
   Organize your treasure hunt into phases. Set reasonable goals for what you want to accomplish each day—whether it's solving a specific riddle, uncovering a new clue, or reaching a particular location. This approach helps you keep the hunt manageable and gives you a sense of accomplishment.

3. **Stay Curious and Open-Minded**
   The greatest treasure hunters are those who stay curious and remain open to different possibilities. A clue might seem unimportant at first, but with a bit of lateral thinking or a change in perspective, it

could reveal the key to the next stage of the journey. Keep questioning and exploring.

Strategies for Success: What You Need to Know

Treasure hunting is not just about following a map and finding hidden riches—it's about employing a strategic approach, staying focused, and using all the resources at your disposal. While the allure of wealth and discovery can drive the hunt, the journey itself is just as important. Success in a treasure hunt depends on the ability to strategize, solve challenges, and stay resilient in the face of obstacles. In this chapter, we will explore the essential strategies that can increase your chances of success in your treasure-hunting adventure.

1. Set Clear Goals and Stay Focused

Before you even begin your treasure hunt, it's crucial to define what success looks like to you. Are you in it for the wealth, the thrill of discovery, or the personal growth that comes with solving complex challenges? Setting clear goals will keep you motivated and focused, especially when the hunt becomes difficult.

How to Set Achievable Goals

Define the Scope:

The first step in setting clear goals is to understand the scope of your hunt. Is the treasure located across several states or within a particular city? Are you hunting for something tangible, like gold, or a more abstract treasure, like a historical artifact? The clearer you are on the boundaries of your search, the more focused your efforts will be.

Break Down Large Goals into Smaller Tasks:

Large goals, like "Find the treasure," can feel overwhelming. Instead, break your mission down into smaller, manageable steps. This could be as simple as "Decode the first clue" or "Reach the marked location" or "Identify the landmark referenced in the riddle." By accomplishing small tasks, you'll make incremental progress, and the overall goal will feel more attainable.

Measure Progress:

Keep track of your progress as you go. Document your findings, observations, and changes in your plans. Monitoring your progress helps you see where you are succeeding and where adjustments need to be made. Plus, it will help you identify patterns, mark milestones, and track any clues you've missed.

2. Master the Art of Research

A successful treasure hunt is rooted in research. Treasure maps, historical references, riddles, and clues all have a backstory that can guide your search. Research is the foundation that connects the dots between the present day and the past, providing context and filling in crucial details.

How to Conduct Effective Research

Dive Into History:

Understanding the history behind the treasure, the people who hid it, and the cultural context is critical. For instance, if the treasure you're seeking is connected to a historical figure like Amelia Earhart, researching her life, journey, and known locations will help you identify potential clues and locations.

Use Multiple Sources:

Research is rarely straightforward, especially when it comes to treasure hunting. Don't rely on just one source—cross-reference historical documents, local legends, academic texts, and online resources. Interviews with experts, such as historians, archaeologists, and even local residents, can provide invaluable insights.

Stay Updated:

Treasure hunts evolve as new information is discovered. Stay up to date with recent findings, news, or breakthroughs that might impact your search. Many famous treasure hunts, such as the Forrest Fenn treasure, have continued to provide new clues or even partial solutions over time.

Analyze Old Maps and Documents:

Ancient maps and documents often hold the key to solving treasure hunts. Analyze these resources closely for symbols, language, and markers that may reveal hidden meanings. If you are unfamiliar with old cartography, seek out an expert in ancient manuscripts or maps who can help you interpret them correctly.

3. Be Methodical in Your Approach

Treasure hunts are rarely linear. You might encounter unexpected obstacles or find yourself retracing your steps after a clue leads to a dead-end. Being methodical in your approach allows you to adapt to the twists and turns, and ensures that you don't miss critical details.

How to Be Methodical

Create a Plan of Action:

Before you set out, create a detailed plan that outlines your steps for each stage of the hunt. Consider the resources you need, the tools to bring, the terrain, and any weather-related factors that might affect your progress.

Take One Step at a Time:

Don't rush through the process. While it might be tempting to chase every potential lead or follow every clue immediately, being too hasty can cause you to overlook important details. Instead, focus on one task at a time, whether that's decoding a clue or exploring a new location.

Stay Organized:

Organizing your notes, maps, and clues is essential. Whether you use a notebook, digital tool, or even a map, make sure all the information you collect is well-organized. You might need to refer back to earlier clues or re-analyze patterns that seemed irrelevant at the time. Staying organized ensures you don't lose important leads.

Be Patient:

Treasure hunting is not a race. It's a journey that requires patience, persistence, and careful consideration. If you find yourself stuck or overwhelmed, take a step back and reevaluate. Sometimes, stepping away from a problem for a while can give you a fresh perspective.

4. Use Technology to Your Advantage

In today's world, treasure hunters have access to a wealth of technological tools that can significantly improve their chances of success. From mapping software to satellite imagery, there are a variety of resources available that can make your hunt more efficient and productive.

Tech Tools for Treasure Hunters

Geospatial Mapping Software:

Mapping software can help you analyze topographical features, create digital maps, and even track your progress. These tools allow you to pinpoint specific locations, cross-reference with historical data, and get a broader view of the search area. For treasure hunts that involve large regions or complex locations, this software can be invaluable.

GPS and Digital Compass:

A GPS device will help you navigate to precise locations, especially when coordinates are involved in the hunt. Pair this with a digital compass to ensure you stay oriented and on the right track.

Satellite Imagery:

Services like Google Earth or specialized satellite imagery can help you identify key geographic features, such as roads, water sources, and landmarks that might be relevant to your treasure map. High-resolution satellite imagery can also reveal changes in the landscape, like hidden caves, paths, or unusual formations.

Document and Image Analysis Tools:

If your treasure map involves images or documents with hidden clues (such as watermarks, faint inscriptions, or coded messages), digital tools like Photoshop or text recognition software can help you uncover elements that aren't immediately visible to the naked eye.

5. Trust Your Instincts and Stay Resilient

While knowledge, strategy, and tools are essential for treasure hunting, your intuition and mental resilience play a key role in navigating the challenges you'll face along the way. Sometimes, treasure hunts can become frustrating or long-winded, and it's easy to feel discouraged. Resilience and a positive mindset can keep you going.

How to Cultivate Resilience and Trust Your Instincts

Trust Your Gut:

Sometimes, the treasure hunt doesn't follow a clear path. When you find yourself stuck or unsure, trust your instincts. If a clue feels significant or a location feels promising, follow it. Often, intuition is built on subconscious knowledge and pattern recognition that you might not fully understand at the time.

Stay Positive:

The hunt will present obstacles—whether it's harsh weather, elusive clues, or physical exhaustion. Maintaining a positive attitude will help you push through setbacks. Remember, many treasure hunts aren't won on the first try. Success is built on perseverance.

Learn from Failure:

Every failure is an opportunity to learn. Whether you misunderstood a clue or took a wrong turn, each misstep provides valuable insights. The more you experience, the better equipped you'll be to handle future challenges. Failure is not the end of the road—it's simply part of the journey.

Treasure hunting requires more than just a lucky break—it demands preparation, strategy, and persistence. By setting clear goals, conducting thorough research, being methodical in your approach, leveraging technology, and trusting your instincts, you can dramatically increase your chances of success. The true treasure lies not only in the riches you might find but in the skills, insights, and resilience you develop along the way. As you embark on your journey, remember that every step, no matter how small, is part of the adventure. Keep moving forward, stay focused, and who knows—you may just uncover the treasure waiting for you.

The Treasure of Personal Growth

Beyond Material Wealth: The Treasures Within

While the treasure hunt may be focused on tangible riches—gold, rare artifacts, or historical treasures—there is an even greater, more valuable treasure to be discovered along the journey: **personal growth**. As you embark on this thrilling quest to uncover hidden fortunes, you will encounter challenges that will test your perseverance, adaptability, and inner strength. These challenges, in turn, will reveal the richest rewards of all—the treasures that lie within you.

In this chapter, we will explore how the pursuit of treasure can lead to deeper insights into who you are, how you grow, and what truly matters in life. Beyond the external bounty, it is the internal transformation that proves to be the most lasting and meaningful treasure.

---

1. The Power of Persistence: Building Resilience Through the Hunt

Treasure hunting is a journey of persistence. Whether you're deciphering a complex riddle, navigating difficult terrain, or revisiting the same location multiple times in search of new clues, the path is rarely straightforward. Every step forward comes with its own setbacks, but each challenge brings an opportunity to strengthen one of the most vital qualities for personal growth—resilience.

How Persistence Shapes Personal Growth

- **Learning to Overcome Adversity**: Treasure hunts require overcoming adversity, be it physical exhaustion, mental fatigue, or frustration from not finding immediate success. Each obstacle faced and surpassed is a testament to your inner strength. Every failure is not the end but a stepping stone to greater self-confidence and determination.

- **Cultivating Patience**: The slow and steady progress you make in a treasure hunt builds patience—a valuable skill that extends far beyond the treasure quest. In real life, patience helps you navigate through challenging situations, whether in personal relationships or in your professional life.

- **Developing Mental Toughness**: Persistence teaches mental fortitude. When faced with dead ends or overwhelming odds, the ability to keep going, to "push through," builds mental resilience. This trait is essential for tackling any of life's difficulties, from personal struggles to career challenges.

2. Problem-Solving: Unlocking Your Inner Detective

Treasure hunts are puzzles—intricate, complex, and designed to challenge your reasoning and problem-solving skills. Solving clues, unraveling riddles, and piecing together disparate pieces of information require a keen mind, logical thinking, and creativity. Along the way, you'll learn that the ability to think critically and approach problems from various angles is a treasure in itself.

How Problem-Solving Fuels Personal Growth

- **Enhancing Critical Thinking**: Each riddle or challenge you face forces you to think critically. You learn to analyze situations more deeply, consider multiple possibilities, and assess the consequences of your decisions. In life, this translates to better decision-making, allowing you to approach problems with a clearer, more objective mindset.

- **Strengthening Creativity**: Sometimes, finding the right solution involves thinking outside the box. The treasure hunt encourages you to be inventive and to trust your intuition when faced with ambiguous situations. Creativity becomes a tool not just for solving clues, but for overcoming obstacles in life, from creative endeavors to finding innovative solutions in the workplace.

- **Boosting Confidence in Problem-Solving**: As you crack codes and uncover hidden meanings, you gain confidence in your problem-solving abilities. Each success, big or small, reinforces your belief that you can handle future challenges with ease. This confidence radiates beyond the hunt itself and empowers you to tackle new challenges in all areas of your life.

---

3. Emotional Growth: The Lessons Hidden in the Journey

The journey of treasure hunting can be an emotional rollercoaster—moments of triumph, setbacks, frustration, and elation. These experiences not only teach you about external obstacles but also about yourself and your emotional responses. You will likely encounter moments when you're forced to confront your fears, doubts, and insecurities. It's through facing these emotional challenges that you will experience profound personal growth.

How Emotional Growth Translates to Success

- **Managing Emotions Under Pressure**: Whether you're racing against the clock to find a hidden item or grappling with a challenging puzzle, you'll need to manage your emotions under pressure. The ability to remain calm, focused, and composed in stressful situations is a powerful skill that will benefit you in high-stakes environments, from work to personal relationships.

- **Building Empathy and Self-Awareness**: Throughout the journey, you will inevitably encounter others on their own treasure hunts. Collaboration, competition, or even simply interacting with people along the way will help you build empathy and improve your interpersonal skills. Understanding the emotions of others, as well as your own, is crucial for building strong relationships and personal growth.

- **Conquering Fear**: The fear of failure, the fear of not succeeding, or the fear of making mistakes is a universal experience. The treasure hunt encourages you to face and overcome these fears head-on. Every time you take a risk, challenge yourself, or step out of your comfort zone, you're learning how to conquer fear and build confidence in your ability to handle uncertainty.

---

4. Growth Through Failure: Turning Setbacks into Stepping Stones

Failure is an inevitable part of any treasure hunt. There will be moments when you miss a clue, misinterpret a symbol, or fall short of a goal. But failure isn't a dead end—it's an opportunity for growth. In fact, failure may be one of the greatest treasures on the journey.

How Failure Contributes to Personal Growth

- **Learning from Mistakes**: Each failure presents a lesson. When a clue leads you in the wrong direction or when a method doesn't work as expected, the experience provides valuable insights. What went wrong? What could you do differently? Through this reflection, you refine your approach, hone your skills, and come back even stronger.

- **Building Resilience Through Setbacks**: As you encounter obstacles, you'll find that resilience is built in the face of adversity. How you react to setbacks defines your ability to move forward. The treasure hunt teaches that failure is not a reason to give up, but a motivator to try again—this mindset is invaluable in all areas of life.

- **Developing a Growth Mindset**: Embracing failure is essential to adopting a growth mindset. Treasure hunting teaches you that growth is continuous, and that success is often just the culmination of many small lessons learned along the way. Every failure becomes an opportunity for self-improvement.

5. The Treasure of Gratitude: Finding Joy in the Journey

While the ultimate treasure may be a material prize, the true essence of the treasure hunt is not found in the final discovery, but in the journey itself. Along the way, you'll encounter breathtaking landscapes, historical moments, and meaningful experiences that enrich your life. Learning to appreciate these moments and cultivating gratitude will transform your perspective and bring greater joy to your life.

How Gratitude Enriches Personal Growth

- **Appreciating the Present**: In the rush to find the treasure, it's easy to overlook the present moment. However, the journey is full of small, significant moments—unexpected discoveries, personal insights, or moments of beauty. Learning to savor these moments will help you appreciate life beyond just the end goal.

- **Building Positive Relationships**: Gratitude also nurtures relationships. Whether you're collaborating with fellow treasure hunters or connecting with local experts, expressing gratitude strengthens bonds and builds goodwill. Gratitude is contagious, and fostering it enriches not only your journey but also your life.

- **Finding Fulfillment in the Process**: Ultimately, the most valuable treasure may be the personal growth you experience along the way. Gratitude helps you see that the process of discovery—the challenges, the lessons, and the growth—is just as precious as the treasure itself. This mindset allows you to find fulfillment regardless of the material wealth you gain.

A Richer Treasure Beyond Wealth

As you embark on your treasure hunt, remember that the greatest treasure you can find is not something you can hold in your hands, but something that lives within you: personal growth. The skills you develop, the resilience you cultivate, and the emotional and intellectual growth you experience will stay with you long after the hunt ends. Whether or not you discover the riches hidden in the map, you will find that the treasure within—your ability to persevere, learn, grow, and find joy in the process—is far more valuable than any material wealth.

In the end, the treasure hunt is not just about what you find, but who you become along the way. Keep your heart and mind open to the journey, and you may uncover a wealth far beyond anything you could have imagined.

Love, Joy, and Understanding: The True Riches of Life

As you embark on the treasure hunt to uncover hidden riches—gold, rare artifacts, and historical treasures—it's easy to become focused on the tangible rewards. The thrill of discovery, the excitement of unearthing something valuable, can be intoxicating. However, as you navigate the clues and challenges, it's important to recognize that there are treasures far more precious than any physical item: **love**, **joy**, and **understanding**. These intangible treasures form the core of human experience, and in many ways, they are the truest riches in life.

In this chapter, we will explore how the pursuit of external wealth can illuminate the deeper treasures that lie within the heart and soul. Through the process of self-discovery, facing challenges, and connecting with others, you will find that love, joy, and understanding are the most enduring and meaningful forms of wealth. These treasures cannot be stolen, lost, or diminished; they grow within you and enrich your life in ways no material possession can.

---

1. Love: The Foundation of True Wealth

Love is often referred to as the most powerful force in the world, and for good reason. It is the bedrock upon which all meaningful human connections are built. In the context of the treasure hunt, love is not just about romantic affection, but about deep empathy, connection, and care—for yourself, others, and the world around you.

How Love Enhances Your Life

- **Love for Yourself**: The treasure hunt may push you to confront your fears, doubts, and insecurities, making it an ideal opportunity for self-love and acceptance. True personal growth starts with loving and accepting who you are—imperfections, flaws, and all. When you embrace your true self, you unlock a confidence and strength that will propel you forward, both in the hunt and in life.

- **Love for Others**: As you meet fellow treasure hunters, local guides, and strangers along your journey, love manifests as empathy and kindness. These connections, whether fleeting or lasting, enrich the treasure hunt experience. Love fosters collaboration, generosity, and mutual respect, and in these interactions, you will often find the most rewarding aspects of life—not a treasure chest of gold, but a treasure trove of human connection.

- **Love for the Journey**: When you approach the treasure hunt with a mindset of love, you begin to cherish every moment, even the challenges. You learn to appreciate the process, not just the outcome. Love for the journey means finding meaning in each step, savoring the lessons, and embracing the unexpected detours along the way. This mindset transforms the hunt into a life-affirming adventure, rather than a mere quest for wealth.

2. Joy: The True Treasure of the Heart

Joy is the emotional currency of life. Unlike fleeting happiness or temporary pleasure, joy is a deep, abiding sense of contentment and fulfillment that comes from living authentically, with purpose, and in harmony with the world. It is the treasure that emerges when you align your actions, values, and passions, and it often arises in the most unexpected places, especially during the pursuit of a greater purpose.

How Joy Transforms Your Journey

- **Finding Joy in Small Moments**: During the treasure hunt, the greatest joys often come not from finding the treasure itself but from the little moments along the way. Whether it's a quiet moment of reflection after solving a difficult clue, the thrill of discovering a hidden location, or the joy of shared laughter with fellow seekers, these small joys add up to create a fulfilling experience. Learning to appreciate these moments is a key part of the treasure hunt, as it trains you to find joy in every step of life.

- **The Joy of Giving**: Often, the most joy comes from giving rather than receiving. Throughout the treasure hunt, you may find yourself sharing your knowledge, helping others, or contributing to a cause greater than yourself. Giving not only brings joy to others but also nurtures a sense of purpose and fulfillment in your own life. The treasure of joy multiplies when shared with those around you.

- **Joy Through Growth**: As you confront challenges, solve riddles, and grow through the experience, you will discover that true joy is born of personal evolution. Each breakthrough, each lesson learned, adds another layer to your inner happiness. The more you grow as a person, the more joy you experience, not just in the successes, but in the process of becoming the best version of yourself.

---

3. Understanding: The Treasure of Insight and Connection

While the pursuit of material wealth can often focus on accumulation, true richness comes from understanding—understanding yourself, others, and the world around you. Understanding enables connection, fosters empathy, and allows you to see beyond surface-level interactions. It's the ability to look deeper into the essence of things, to ask questions and seek meaning, that makes life truly rich.

How Understanding Deepens Your Life

- **Self-Understanding**: One of the most profound rewards of the treasure hunt is the opportunity it offers for introspection. As you navigate through clues and face challenges, you may begin to uncover hidden aspects of yourself—your strengths, fears, desires, and motivations. Understanding yourself at a deeper level brings clarity and peace, allowing you to make decisions that align with your values and your true purpose.

- **Understanding Others**: The relationships you build throughout the treasure hunt—whether with other hunters or locals who assist you—offer a chance to cultivate a greater understanding of others. Empathy grows when you listen, connect, and appreciate the perspectives and experiences of those around you. This understanding helps you form deeper, more meaningful relationships and enriches your life far more than any material possession could.

- **Understanding the World**: The treasure hunt is a journey not just of discovery, but of learning. Along the way, you will gain insights into history, art, culture, and geography. This knowledge deepens your connection to the world and enhances your appreciation of the interconnectedness of all things. As you gain understanding, you realize that the treasure you seek is part of a larger story—one that stretches across time, space, and humanity.

4. Living a Life of True Wealth: Cultivating Love, Joy, and Understanding

As you continue on your treasure hunt, remember that love, joy, and understanding are the true treasures of life. These riches are not bound by time or space, nor can they be taken from you. They are the core of human existence, and by nurturing them, you create a life that is rich beyond measure.

How to Cultivate These Treasures

- **Practice Gratitude**: Gratitude is the foundation of love, joy, and understanding. By recognizing and appreciating the beauty in life's simple moments, you cultivate a mindset that invites more love and joy into your life. Gratitude enhances understanding, helping you see the world through a lens of appreciation rather than entitlement.

- **Invest in Relationships**: The most meaningful wealth is often found in the relationships you nurture. Whether it's through family, friends, or the community you build, investing in others allows love, joy, and understanding to flourish. These connections are the treasures that remain with you long after material riches fade.

- **Pursue a Life of Purpose**: When you live with intention, guided by your values and passions, love, joy, and understanding naturally flow into your life.

This treasure hunt is not just a pursuit of external wealth, but a journey toward living a life that reflects your highest ideals and deepest truths.

Stories of Transformation: How Treasure Hunts Change Us

The allure of hidden treasures has captivated human imagination for centuries, from the legendary stories of pirates' gold to modern-day hunts for rare artifacts. The quest for treasure is more than just a physical pursuit—it's a journey of transformation. As treasure hunters embark on their adventures, they often discover something far more valuable than what lies at the end of their search: **themselves**. Treasure hunts, whether literal or metaphorical, have the power to reshape us in profound ways.

In this chapter, we explore **how the process of hunting for treasure**—uncovering clues, overcoming obstacles, and following elusive leads—can lead to **personal growth, emotional resilience, and life-altering transformations**. Along the way, we will share stories of individuals whose lives were forever changed by their own treasure hunts, illustrating how the pursuit of hidden riches can lead to deeper self-understanding, new relationships, and lasting fulfillment.

1. The Adventure of Self-Discovery

One of the most profound transformations that occur during a treasure hunt is the discovery of the self. As individuals engage in the pursuit of a goal—whether it's financial gain, historical exploration, or personal challenge—they are often forced to confront their deepest fears, aspirations, and limitations. The journey, with its obstacles and successes, offers an opportunity for growth that transcends material rewards.

Example: The Inner Journey of a Treasure Hunter

Take the story of **Sarah**, a young woman who embarked on a treasure hunt after a period of personal loss and stagnation. Initially, Sarah's goal was to find a hidden cache of rare historical artifacts, believing that material success would heal her emotional wounds. However, as she worked through the physical challenges of the hunt, solving riddles and deciphering clues, she began to discover something much more important—**her own inner strength**.

With each challenge she overcame, Sarah grew more confident in her abilities. The long hours of contemplation, coupled with moments of failure and success, taught her resilience and patience. Eventually, Sarah realized that the real treasure she was seeking wasn't just a collection of artifacts, but **her own sense of self-worth**. The hunt had led her to a deeper understanding of her inner strength and emotional endurance, teaching her that the most valuable discoveries are often those that can't be seen with the eyes but felt deeply within.

2. The Power of Overcoming Obstacles

Treasure hunts are never without their challenges—whether it's deciphering an ancient puzzle, braving dangerous terrain, or competing with other hunters. Each obstacle becomes a lesson in perseverance, problem-solving, and adaptability. The process of overcoming these challenges often brings out the best in people, revealing untapped reserves of creativity, determination, and problem-solving skills.

Example: A Treasure Hunt That Transformed a Relationship

In another story, **David** and his son **Ethan** embarked on a treasure hunt together, hoping it would be a fun bonding experience. What began as a way to reconnect soon became a test of their relationship. Along the way, they faced numerous setbacks, including misinterpretation of clues, bad weather, and physical exhaustion. Tensions mounted as David's frustration grew, while Ethan struggled to find his confidence in a world of adult decisions and responsibilities.

However, through the process of solving the challenges together, the duo's relationship began to shift. They began to communicate more effectively, recognizing each other's strengths and learning to rely on one another. When they eventually uncovered the final treasure, the real reward was the **reconnection of their bond**—something that would have never happened had they not persevered through the adversity of the hunt.

The hunt, while full of material promise, became a **transformative journey** that taught them patience, empathy, and the power of cooperation. In the end, the treasure they unearthed wasn't just the tangible prize—it was the new depth of understanding and connection they had created between father and son.

---

3. The Quest for Purpose and Meaning

For some, a treasure hunt represents a search for more than just riches—it is a quest for deeper meaning, purpose, and fulfillment. In the pursuit of something larger than oneself, hunters are often driven to examine their core beliefs, values, and motivations, which can lead to profound transformations in how they view their lives and their place in the world.

Example: A Man's Search for Significance

James, a middle-aged corporate executive, found himself feeling disconnected from his work and family life. After decades of chasing financial success and career advancement, he realized that he felt empty inside, disconnected from any meaningful purpose. When James heard about an obscure treasure hunt that promised to uncover artifacts tied to world history, he decided to give it a try—not out of a desire for wealth, but to **rediscover his sense of purpose**.

Throughout the hunt, James encountered not only intellectual challenges but also moments of profound reflection. The historical significance of the treasures he uncovered—pieces of art, ancient relics, and artifacts with deep stories—sparked an awakening within him. The more he learned about history, culture, and the lives of those who had come before him, the more he felt connected to something greater than himself.

By the end of the hunt, James had not only discovered valuable objects but had also **rediscovered his own sense of significance** in the larger tapestry of life. The experience reshaped his perspective on success, leading him to pursue a new career in education, where he could share his passion for history and contribute to something that truly mattered. The treasure he found was not in the objects he uncovered, but in the newfound meaning he brought back into his life.

---

4. Finding the True Treasure: Relationships and Connection

While the primary goal of a treasure hunt might be to uncover riches or historical items, the relationships and connections formed during the journey often become the most valuable treasures of all. The camaraderie, teamwork, and shared experiences among fellow hunters forge lasting bonds that have the power to change lives in unexpected ways.

Example: Lifelong Friendships Born of a Hunt

Take the case of **Mark** and **Tina**, two strangers who met while searching for a hidden treasure in a remote mountain range. Despite coming from vastly different backgrounds—Mark was a seasoned outdoorsman, while Tina was a beginner with limited knowledge of treasure hunting—they quickly became a team. Through their time spent together, facing physical hardships and solving challenging puzzles, they developed a **deep, lasting friendship** built on mutual respect and shared goals.

Over the years, Mark and Tina continued to travel together, embark on new hunts, and support each other through personal and professional challenges. What started as a competitive treasure hunt soon transformed into a lifelong friendship based on shared experiences and a mutual appreciation for one another's unique qualities.

In many ways, this story demonstrates that the treasure hunt is as much about **human connection** as it is about material wealth. Through these interactions, we uncover treasures that cannot be measured in dollars or artifacts—but in the profound relationships and the collective wisdom they bring into our lives.

---

5. Transforming the World: How Treasure Hunts Lead to Social Change

While the personal transformations that occur through treasure hunts are powerful, the effects of these hunts often extend far beyond the individual. Many treasure hunters are motivated by the idea that their discoveries can contribute to a larger cause, whether through supporting charitable efforts, preserving history, or advocating for environmental protection.

Example: Treasure Hunts for Good

One notable example of this is the story of **The Hidden Treasure of Sustainability**, a modern treasure hunt designed not only to uncover hidden artifacts but to promote environmental stewardship. Organized by a nonprofit dedicated to sustainability, the hunt encouraged participants to find buried treasures that contained rare seeds, pieces of renewable energy technology, or instructions for creating sustainable living environments.

For many participants, the hunt became more than a race for material wealth—it was a **quest for social impact**. The knowledge and technologies uncovered during the hunt led to innovative solutions for reducing carbon footprints, supporting local communities, and protecting endangered species. This shift in mindset demonstrated how a treasure hunt could lead not only to personal transformation but to positive change on a global scale.

The Journey of Discovery

Tales of Real-Life Treasure Hunts

The quest for treasure has been a defining aspect of human history, driving explorers, adventurers, and ordinary people alike to embark on thrilling journeys filled with mystery and wonder. From ancient civilizations to modern-day adventurers, the pursuit of hidden riches has fueled some of the most captivating and transformative stories ever told. In this chapter, we delve into real-life treasure hunts that have captured the imagination of people around the world, each one offering valuable lessons about perseverance, discovery, and the human spirit.

These tales are not just about the treasures themselves— they are about the people who sought them, the obstacles they faced, and the profound impact these hunts had on their lives. Each journey is a testament to the power of curiosity, the thrill of adventure, and the unexpected ways in which treasure hunts can lead to both external discoveries and inner transformation.

1. The Forrest Fenn Treasure Hunt: A Modern Legend

One of the most famous treasure hunts of the 21st century is the story of Forrest Fenn's hidden treasure. Fenn, a Santa Fe art dealer and collector, claimed to have hidden a chest filled with gold, gems, and other valuable artifacts somewhere in the Rocky Mountains in 2010. The treasure was said to be worth over $2 million, and Fenn's clues, scattered throughout his memoir The Thrill of the Chase, became the foundation for an adventurous nationwide hunt.

For over a decade, treasure hunters from around the world scoured the vast wilderness, deciphering cryptic riddles, battling harsh environments, and forging bonds along the way. The hunt took on a life of its own, inspiring online communities and global media coverage, as people dedicated years of their lives to solving Fenn's clues.

In June 2020, Fenn announced that the treasure had been found by an anonymous hunter, but not before the hunt had inspired countless people to embark on their own journeys of discovery. For many, the Forrest Fenn treasure hunt was about more than just the riches—it became a quest for meaning, a chance to connect with nature, and an opportunity to experience the thrill of chasing a dream. Though some hunters never found the treasure, many came away from the journey with new friendships, a renewed sense of adventure, and valuable personal growth.

2. The Oak Island Mystery: The Curse of Hidden Riches

The legend of Oak Island, located off the coast of Nova Scotia, Canada, is one of the oldest and most enduring treasure hunts in history. For over 200 years, treasure seekers have scoured the island, trying to uncover a hidden treasure believed to be buried deep within its mysterious "Money Pit." Some believe the treasure to be the lost hoard of pirates, while others speculate it could be the fabled treasure of the Knights Templar.

Despite numerous excavations and countless attempts to uncover the treasure, the island's mysteries remain unsolved, fueling speculation and intrigue. Throughout the centuries, treasure hunters have faced a series of mysterious setbacks—unexpected flooding, cave-ins, and even deaths—that have led some to believe that the island is cursed. But despite these setbacks, the hunt persists, with teams of modern-day explorers continuing to dig into the depths of the island, each new discovery offering tantalizing glimpses of what might lie beneath.

The Oak Island treasure hunt is unique not only because of the centuries-long mystery but also because of the rich history and folklore surrounding it. The stories of explorers, failed expeditions, and lost hopes have become an integral part of the legend, with each new chapter in the hunt further solidifying Oak Island as a symbol of both perseverance and the human fascination with the unknown. Whether the treasure is ever found or not, the hunt itself serves as a reminder that sometimes the true treasure is in the journey rather than the destination.

3. The Hunt for the Nazi Gold Train: A Tale of Lost Riches

In the aftermath of World War II, rumors began circulating that a train loaded with gold and other treasures had been hidden by Nazi soldiers somewhere in the mountains of Poland. The legend of the "Nazi Gold Train" has fascinated treasure hunters for decades, with countless expeditions launched to locate the lost train, which was believed to have been hidden in a network of underground tunnels near the town of Walbrzych.

The legend gained renewed attention in 2015 when two treasure hunters claimed to have found the train's location, sparking a renewed interest in the search. Despite multiple expeditions, the elusive treasure has never been recovered, and the mystery surrounding the Nazi Gold Train endures.

What makes this hunt particularly intriguing is the combination of historical significance and the emotional weight of the lost riches. The idea that the gold could be linked to the spoils of war and human suffering adds a layer of complexity to the search. For many treasure hunters, the pursuit of the Nazi Gold Train is not just about wealth but about uncovering a part of history, perhaps shedding light on one of the darkest chapters of the 20th century.

Though the gold remains hidden, the story of the Nazi Gold Train serves as a reminder of the power of myth and mystery to drive people to search for the past. The hunt is still ongoing, with treasure hunters determined to uncover the truth—no matter how long it takes.

4. The Legend of the Lost Dutchman's Gold Mine

The Lost Dutchman's Gold Mine is one of the most famous and enduring treasure legends in the American Southwest. According to legend, a German immigrant named Jacob Waltz discovered a rich gold mine in the Superstition Mountains of Arizona in the 19th century. Before his death, Waltz reportedly shared clues about the mine's location with a close friend, but the treasure was never found, and the mystery of its whereabouts has captivated treasure hunters ever since.

Over the years, numerous people have claimed to have found the mine or discovered valuable gold in the area, but no one has ever confirmed the existence of the treasure. The hunt for the Lost Dutchman's Mine has become legendary, with explorers braving the rugged Arizona wilderness in search of the elusive treasure. Along the way, many have faced harsh conditions, such as extreme heat, treacherous terrain, and even disappearances.

The story of the Lost Dutchman's Mine is wrapped in legend and superstition, with some believing that the treasure is cursed, and those who seek it are doomed to fail. Despite these warnings, the hunt continues, and the mine remains one of the most tantalizing unsolved mysteries in American folklore.

For many, the Lost Dutchman's Gold Mine is more than just a treasure—it represents the spirit of adventure, the thrill of the unknown, and the belief that there is still treasure waiting to be uncovered in the wild corners of the world.

5. The Great Emu War Treasure: A Lost Hoard in Australia

The story of the Great Emu War Treasure is lesser known but equally fascinating. In the early 1930s, the Australian government offered a bounty on emus—large flightless birds that were destroying crops in Western Australia. The result was a bizarre and often humorous military campaign known as the "Emu War." However, among the aftermath of the war, there are rumors of a hidden treasure, said to be buried by the soldiers involved in the failed campaign.

While the story itself might seem a bit odd, it is a reminder that treasure hunts can come from the most unexpected of places. Over the years, adventurers have scoured the Australian outback in search of the hidden hoard, which is believed to be buried near the sites where the soldiers once camped. Though no treasure has been found to date, the Great Emu War treasure hunt illustrates how even seemingly trivial events can give rise to legends, myths, and real-life treasure quests.

The Adventure of Pursuing Dreams

The pursuit of dreams is often described as a journey—one that is as rewarding as it is challenging, filled with triumphs, setbacks, and moments of profound transformation. This adventure is not merely about the destination but about the courage it takes to begin, the resilience required to persevere, and the discoveries made along the way. Whether the dream is big or small, personal or professional, the pursuit of one's aspirations brings with it a sense of purpose that can lead to self-discovery, growth, and a deeper understanding of the world around us.

In this exploration, we'll examine how the adventure of pursuing dreams mirrors the treasure hunts and quests we've discussed: both involve risk, dedication, hope, and a deep belief that something meaningful lies ahead. But pursuing dreams, like any great adventure, is ultimately a journey toward **the best version of ourselves**.

---

1. The Call to Adventure: Identifying Your Dream

Every great adventure begins with a call. In the context of pursuing dreams, this call is the spark—the moment when you recognize what it is you truly desire to achieve, experience, or contribute. Whether it's a career goal, a personal passion, or a vision for the future, this dream is often something that stirs your heart and mind, pushing you to take the first step.

But before embarking on this journey, it's important to identify and define the dream clearly. This might require introspection, self-reflection, and a willingness to confront the uncertainties that often accompany the unknown. Much like treasure hunters who first hear whispers of buried riches, we too must often embark on a search to uncover what truly excites and motivates us.

For some, the call is obvious, while for others, it may require time to listen deeply and carefully to one's desires. The key is to take that first step, even if it feels intimidating. Just like a treasure map, your dreams may come with uncertainty and confusion at the start, but it's that uncertainty that often makes the journey so worthwhile. By answering the call, you're committing to the adventure of **self-discovery** and **personal growth**.

---

2. Facing Obstacles: The Trials and Challenges

No adventure is without its obstacles, and the pursuit of a dream is no exception. Along the way, we face various trials—some of which are expected, others that may catch us off guard. These challenges are not only tests of our willpower but also opportunities for growth and resilience.

Many of us will encounter **self-doubt**: the voice that questions whether our dreams are achievable or whether we are worthy of success. External obstacles, such as financial barriers, lack of support, or societal expectations, may also appear. But it is in overcoming these trials that we come to realize the true value of our dreams. They act as **catalysts for transformation**, forcing us to dig deeper, to learn more about ourselves, and to find strength we didn't know we had.

Think of the treasure hunters who, upon hearing the call to adventure, ventured into harsh wildernesses or treacherous waters. They didn't always succeed immediately. Some failed, some became discouraged, and some turned back. But those who persisted—who remained determincd despite setbacks—were the ones who unlocked the rewards of their efforts. This parallel is key to pursuing our own dreams: **perseverance is the bridge between desire and achievement.**

---

3. Learning and Growing: The Treasure of Self-Discovery

One of the greatest treasures found in the pursuit of dreams is the **self-discovery** that comes along with the journey. Dreams often lead us down paths we never expected, and as we navigate these paths, we learn more about who we are and what we're capable of. Much like treasure hunters who uncover not just gold but hidden talents and wisdom, the pursuit of dreams opens the door to greater understanding and deeper connection with ourselves.

Through the pursuit of a dream, we confront our fears, challenge our limitations, and refine our strengths. We become more attuned to what we value, more aware of what motivates us, and better equipped to handle future challenges. The lessons we learn from our adventures— whether successes or failures—are integral to our **personal evolution**. In a sense, the pursuit of a dream is a treasure hunt for **our true potential**.

4. The Role of Passion and Vision: Guiding the Way

A dream without passion is like a treasure without a map—it lacks direction and purpose. Passion is the fuel that drives us forward when the road becomes tough, and **vision** is the compass that guides us, helping us navigate through periods of uncertainty. These two elements are critical for sustaining momentum, especially when obstacles arise.

Much like treasure hunters who remain focused on their goal despite facing unclear paths and confusing clues, individuals pursuing their dreams must remain connected to their **why**. Passion ensures that even when the path is unclear, we keep moving forward. Vision provides clarity and reminds us of the bigger picture, enabling us to make strategic decisions that align with our ultimate goal.

The journey of pursuing dreams, like any great treasure hunt, is not linear. There will be moments of doubt, but with passion and vision, we find the strength to continue. It's this sense of purpose that helps us tap into the energy required to see our dreams come to fruition.

5. Reaching the Destination: The Reward of Achievement

Finally, the pursuit of dreams leads to the eventual reward—the **realization of a goal**, the unveiling of a long-sought-after treasure. However, much like in the case of treasure hunts, the real reward often extends beyond the material or tangible outcome. While finding the gold may be thrilling, it's the personal growth, resilience, and transformation along the way that offer the most profound riches.

For many, the moment of achievement feels like the culmination of all the hard work, sacrifices, and lessons learned along the journey. Yet, it's also important to remember that the journey itself is an integral part of the reward. The treasure we find in our dreams is not just in the end result but in the transformation that occurs as we chase that dream, face our challenges, and grow through the process.

It's important to celebrate these victories—no matter how big or small—because they are the markers of progress, evidence that the pursuit has been worthwhile. Whether you're an entrepreneur realizing your business dream, an artist completing a project, or someone finally reaching a long-held personal goal, the sense of fulfillment and pride is irreplaceable.

---

6. Continuing the Adventure: New Dreams on the Horizon

As with all great adventures, one treasure hunt often leads to another. Once a dream is realized, many find themselves seeking new challenges, new goals, and new opportunities for growth. The act of pursuing dreams is a lifelong journey—a cycle of discovery, transformation, and reinvention.

The completion of one dream doesn't signify the end of the adventure; rather, it marks the beginning of new possibilities. It is the nature of dreams to evolve, just as treasure hunters find new quests once their original goals are achieved. This continuous cycle of dreaming, pursuing, and achieving ensures that life remains vibrant, dynamic, and full of potential.

How Every Journey is a Treasure Hunt

Life is often compared to a journey—an adventure filled with twists, turns, and unpredictable paths. Much like a treasure hunt, it is a pursuit that invites us to explore the unknown, search for meaning, and discover hidden treasures. These treasures, however, are not always material; they can take the form of wisdom, growth, relationships, and experiences that enrich our lives. Whether we are chasing dreams, seeking fulfillment, or simply trying to navigate through life's complexities, every journey is, in its own way, a treasure hunt.

In this exploration, we will dive into how the journey itself, filled with its challenges, lessons, and rewards, mirrors the essence of a treasure hunt. And just like the most legendary of treasure quests, life's greatest rewards are often found not just in the destination, but in the experiences and transformations that occur along the way.

---

1. The Quest Begins: Answering the Call to Adventure

Every treasure hunt begins with a call to adventure—a moment when we are drawn toward something greater, something unknown. This could be a new goal, a change in direction, or an internal yearning for something more. Similarly, in life, we often experience a call to embark on a journey—whether it's a career shift, a personal project, or a deeper exploration of who we are and what we want from life.

For some, this call is clear and urgent; for others, it's a slow and subtle pull that grows louder over time. It could come in the form of an opportunity, an inspiration, or a life event that awakens something dormant inside. Just like the treasure hunters who, upon hearing rumors of hidden riches, feel the irresistible pull of discovery, we, too, are often compelled to step out of our comfort zones and pursue something bigger.

The decision to embark on a journey—no matter how daunting—is the first step in a transformative adventure. It's a reminder that life itself is not meant to be static, but a dynamic quest where the unknown holds the promise of growth, learning, and self-discovery.

2. The Map: Defining Your Goals and Direction

No treasure hunt is complete without a map—a guide that provides a sense of direction and purpose. Similarly, in life, having a sense of direction or clear goals can serve as our map. This could be a vision for the future, a specific ambition, or a set of values that guide our choices and actions.

Just as treasure hunters study ancient maps to understand the terrain they will face, we, too, must often engage in introspection to define our goals and understand the path ahead. It may not always be clear where the treasure lies, but having a roadmap—whether it's a plan for the next few years, a list of personal values, or a broader vision for what we hope to accomplish—provides us with a framework for the journey.

The treasure map doesn't guarantee a straightforward path. In fact, life's map often comes with detours, obstacles, and confusing paths. But like any great treasure hunt, the map is simply a guide—what truly matters is our willingness to pursue it, even when the terrain is difficult.

3. The Challenges: Overcoming Obstacles and Setbacks

No treasure hunt is without its challenges. Hidden treasures are rarely found easily. Similarly, the pursuit of any meaningful goal or dream involves facing obstacles, setbacks, and periods of uncertainty. Life's greatest rewards are often found through perseverance—by continuing to search even when the treasure seems elusive or the journey feels too difficult.

These challenges can take many forms: external obstacles like financial struggles, societal pressures, or unexpected life events; or internal struggles like fear, self-doubt, or a lack of confidence. Much like treasure hunters who face harsh landscapes, difficult terrain, and the temptation to turn back, we, too, must confront our own fears, limitations, and doubts.

But these challenges are not just barriers; they are the tests that ultimately shape us into who we are meant to become. The resilience we build through overcoming obstacles becomes part of the treasure itself. Like the treasure hunters who, through their determination, eventually discover hidden riches, we, too, find our own rewards in the strength, wisdom, and perseverance we develop along the way.

---

4. The Clues: Learning Along the Way

Treasure hunts are not just about the final destination—they are about the clues we gather along the journey. Every encounter, every piece of wisdom, and every experience offers us insight that brings us closer to our treasure. In life, the journey is a process of **learning**. Each step, each setback, and each moment of success holds a lesson that, when applied, brings us closer to personal fulfillment.

Just like treasure hunters analyze each clue carefully— decoding symbols, reading maps, and interpreting signs— we too must be attuned to the lessons and insights life offers. These clues often come in the form of feedback, experiences, relationships, and moments of self-reflection. Sometimes, these clues are obvious, while other times they are more subtle, hidden beneath layers of experience or emotion.

What makes the journey rich is the act of collecting these clues—learning about ourselves, about others, and about the world around us. With each new piece of wisdom, we gain clarity and understanding, inching closer to the treasure that lies ahead.

5. The Treasure: Finding Fulfillment and Meaning

The treasure at the end of every journey represents the culmination of our efforts, challenges, and discoveries. But it's important to remember that the treasure in life is not always a tangible object or a material goal. Instead, the true treasure lies in the fulfillment we find in the pursuit of our dreams, the growth we experience along the way, and the deeper understanding we gain about ourselves and the world.

For some, the treasure may be a career achievement, a creative accomplishment, or a long-desired personal goal. For others, the treasure could be the relationships wc build, the personal growth we achieve, or the peace we find within ourselves. Just like a treasure hunt, the reward may take different forms for different people, but its value lies in the journey that precedes it.

Even after finding the treasure, the journey doesn't end. Much like treasure hunters who continue to search for new adventures, the pursuit of meaning and fulfillment continues throughout our lives. The process of seeking, growing, and discovering is, in itself, a treasure—a constant reminder that every step in the journey is valuable.

6. The Journey Never Ends: Embracing the Ongoing Adventure

The greatest lesson of any treasure hunt is that the adventure doesn't end when the treasure is found. Similarly, life's journey is not a one-time pursuit but a continual adventure—one that evolves as we do. Once we've reached one treasure, there are always new dreams to pursue, new goals to set, and new challenges to face.

Just as treasure hunters, after discovering one treasure, set off to find new riches, we too find that fulfillment is not a final destination but an ongoing process. Each new phase of life offers fresh opportunities to explore, to grow, and to redefine what our treasure truly is.

Embracing this ongoing adventure means accepting that the journey itself holds infinite value. **The pursuit of meaning, growth, and self-discovery is an ever-evolving treasure hunt**, and it is through these ongoing explorations that we truly unlock the richness of life.

The Legacy of Wealth and Discovery

What You Gain Beyond the Treasure

In every great treasure hunt, there is an inherent allure to the riches promised at the end of the journey. The treasure—whether it's gold, gems, rare collectibles, or life-changing wealth—represents the culmination of years of exploration, effort, and persistence. Yet, as we have seen time and time again throughout history, the true value of a treasure hunt often transcends the material wealth it promises. The legacy of the journey itself—the lessons learned, the relationships formed, the personal growth achieved—becomes the most enduring treasure.

In this chapter, we will explore what you gain beyond the treasure itself. Because in the end, what we truly discover through our pursuit of wealth, success, and discovery is not just the tangible rewards, but the lasting impact of the journey on who we become, how we view the world, and how we shape our legacies for future generations.

1. The Gift of Self-Discovery

The most profound treasure you can discover on any journey is often hidden within yourself. While external riches can bring momentary satisfaction or status, the process of pursuing a dream or uncovering treasure leads to a deeper, more meaningful treasure: **self-discovery**.

As you embark on the treasure hunt of life—whether chasing a professional ambition, seeking personal fulfillment, or even exploring new horizons—each step of the journey encourages introspection and growth. Through challenges and obstacles, we learn more about our own strengths, weaknesses, passions, and resilience. The treasure hunt forces us to ask difficult questions and, in doing so, leads us to uncover truths about who we are and who we aspire to be.

Self-discovery is a gift that continues long after the treasure is found. It shapes how we approach future endeavors, how we respond to adversity, and how we connect with others. The richest treasure is not just in the rewards but in the person we become through the pursuit.

---

2. The Wisdom of Experience

The true wealth of any treasure hunt lies not just in the material goods unearthed but in the **wisdom gained along the way**. Every step taken, every clue deciphered, every challenge faced, brings valuable lessons that stay with you long after the treasure is secured. Life itself is a series of treasure hunts, and each one teaches us something profound about how to navigate the world.

This wisdom comes in many forms:

- **Problem-solving skills**: As you work through the difficulties of the hunt—whether literal or metaphorical—you develop the ability to think critically, make informed decisions, and adapt to changing circumstances.

- **Resilience**: Facing setbacks, whether physical, emotional, or financial, builds your mental fortitude. You learn to overcome adversity and persist even when success seems distant.

- **Patience**: The treasure rarely comes easily. The journey teaches you to be patient with both the process and yourself, understanding that great rewards often take time and effort to manifest.

- **Perspective**: By observing the world through the lens of discovery, you gain a deeper understanding of the people, places, and events that shape your life. You start to see connections between seemingly unrelated aspects of the world, expanding your perspective and understanding.

This wisdom not only enriches your own life but is passed down to others, forming a legacy of knowledge that can guide future generations.

3. The Value of Relationships

While the treasure hunt is often seen as an individual pursuit, it is rarely an isolated journey. Along the way, you encounter a wide variety of people—some may offer help, others may pose challenges, but all contribute to the story of your quest. From mentors and allies to rivals and strangers, the relationships you forge during the treasure hunt are often as valuable as the treasure itself.

When we set out on a personal or professional journey, we inevitably come into contact with others who influence our path. Sometimes, these relationships offer immediate support and guidance, while other times, they challenge us to reconsider our approach or force us to confront uncomfortable truths about ourselves.

The people you meet during your journey leave an imprint on your legacy. These connections have the power to shape who you are and what you become. Collaborative efforts often result in greater achievements, and through shared struggles, we form deep, lasting bonds. Much like the great explorers of history who depended on their teams to find treasure, the connections we make and the bonds we form during our personal pursuits provide a support system that helps us keep moving forward when things get tough.

Moreover, relationships built on trust and mutual respect can form the foundation for even greater endeavors in the future. The exchange of knowledge, ideas, and resources with others enriches the treasure hunt of life in ways that material wealth alone never could.

---

4. The Fulfillment of Legacy

A true legacy goes beyond the treasures you gather in this lifetime. The most significant aspect of any treasure hunt is the legacy it creates—a legacy that **extends beyond material wealth** and into the impact you leave on the world and on the people around you.

Think of the great explorers, innovators, and adventurers in history. Their treasures were not always riches; their real legacy was the ripple effect of their discoveries, the inspiration they provided to others, and the societal changes they ignited. People like **Pablo Picasso**, **Amelia Earhart**, and **George Washington** left behind legacies of transformation—not just for their material wealth or achievements but for the way their journeys impacted the world.

When you embark on your own journey, whether it's to find wealth, build a business, or pursue a dream, consider the broader impact of your actions. **What will you leave behind?** The knowledge you share, the values you impart, and the relationships you build contribute to your legacy and have the potential to inspire and guide others long after you're gone.

A meaningful legacy isn't just about accumulating wealth or achieving recognition; it's about creating something lasting—something that endures and continues to make an impact. The treasure hunt becomes a vehicle for **leaving a mark** that influences others in positive, meaningful ways.

5. The Joy of Contribution

Alongside the pursuit of personal gain comes the **joy of contribution**—the deep satisfaction that comes from knowing that your efforts are not only benefitting yourself but also others. Whether it's through charity, mentorship, or simply being a source of inspiration, the ability to contribute to the well-being of others elevates your journey.

In the context of treasure hunting, there's something deeply fulfilling about sharing discoveries. If we think back to legendary treasure hunts throughout history, those who found riches often shared their fortunes or used their discoveries to benefit society. In the same way, your journey, whether big or small, can benefit others by sharing the lessons learned, the knowledge gained, and the wealth acquired.

This spirit of contribution has the power to **foster a sense of community**, unity, and connection. It encourages people to work together, to support one another, and to create a collective wealth that goes beyond individual pursuit. By giving back and sharing your own treasure—whether material, intellectual, or emotional—you contribute to a cycle of positive change that enriches society as a whole.

---

6. The Treasure of Transformation

Above all, the most enduring treasure you can gain from any journey is **personal transformation**. The treasure hunt is a metaphor for the lifelong process of becoming the person you were always meant to be. Each journey, whether it's seeking wealth, adventure, or purpose, shapes you into a more capable, more aware, and more fulfilled individual.

Through the trials, triumphs, and lessons of the treasure hunt, you transform. You become someone who not only seeks treasures but also understands the deeper meaning of what those treasures represent. The journey changes you— not just on the surface but at your core. This transformation is perhaps the most priceless treasure of all.

Creating a Legacy: The Impact of Your Findings

Treasure hunting is often seen as the pursuit of material wealth, a race to uncover riches hidden in the earth or behind mysterious riddles. However, the true power of treasure hunting goes far beyond finding precious metals, rare artifacts, or vintage collectibles. The ultimate treasure lies in **what you do with what you find**—the lasting legacy you create through your discoveries and the impact you leave on others.

In this section, we will explore the deeper implications of treasure hunting—how the findings, whether tangible or intangible, can shape not only your life but the lives of others. From the ethical considerations of treasure hunting to the ways in which your discoveries can affect your community and future generations, we'll delve into what it means to create a lasting, positive legacy.

---

1. The Power of Sharing Your Findings

When a treasure is uncovered, it's easy to be tempted by the notion of keeping it for oneself. However, **true legacy comes not from hoarding wealth, but from sharing it**. The impact of your discoveries can multiply exponentially when shared with others. Whether you find physical wealth, knowledge, or wisdom, the act of sharing your findings with those around you can create ripples that extend far beyond your immediate circle.

- **Historical treasures**: When you find objects with cultural, historical, or artistic significance, consider how their discovery might benefit society. These objects tell a story, represent a lost chapter of history, and can inspire future generations. By sharing these treasures with museums, collectors, or the public, you ensure that these pieces of history remain accessible and meaningful for years to come.

- **Intellectual treasures**: The knowledge and wisdom gained from a treasure hunt can be just as valuable as material wealth. Whether it's a new theory, a business innovation, or personal insights, sharing this knowledge can help others navigate their own paths. Teaching, writing, or speaking about what you've learned empowers others to take what you have found and apply it to their own journeys.

- **Personal growth**: As you progress through your own journey, you may gain personal insights and self-improvement that others can benefit from. These discoveries about resilience, patience, or perseverance can inspire those around you to embark on their own quests of personal transformation.

By sharing your findings and the lessons they bring, you not only contribute to your community but ensure that the treasure you've uncovered doesn't end with you—it continues to inspire, teach, and impact others.

---

2. The Ethics of Treasure Hunting: Responsibility and Impact

As with any pursuit that involves uncovering hidden or valuable resources, **treasure hunting carries with it a significant ethical responsibility**. When we embark on a treasure hunt, we must consider the potential impact of our findings on others, especially if those findings belong to a wider community or hold historical significance.

- **Respect for history**: Many treasures are more than just physical items; they represent pieces of history, culture, and identity. If you uncover historical treasures, it's important to approach them with the utmost respect and consider their place in the broader historical narrative. This means working with historians, archaeologists, and cultural experts to understand the context of what you've found and ensuring it is preserved for future generations.

- **Environmental impact**: Some treasure hunts take place in natural settings, such as underwater shipwrecks or archaeological digs. In these cases, it's crucial to ensure that your activities don't harm the environment. Ethical treasure hunters prioritize sustainability, working to minimize damage to ecosystems and considering how their actions can impact the local community and wildlife.

- **Ownership and provenance**: Who truly owns a treasure? This question is often debated in the world of treasure hunting. Many treasures, particularly those of significant historical value, are contested—

especially if they have been lost, stolen, or passed down through generations. Ethical treasure hunters take care to investigate the provenance of their findings and act with integrity, ensuring that their discoveries are rightfully claimed and appropriately distributed.

Creating a legacy through treasure hunting involves more than simply uncovering something valuable; it's about **doing so in a way that respects the interests of others, upholds ethical standards, and contributes positively to society.**

---

3. The Ripple Effect: How Your Findings Influence Future Generations

The legacy of treasure hunting doesn't end when the final clue is solved or the treasure chest is opened. Instead, the **impact of your findings** can echo across time and generations, creating a ripple effect that influences the way future generations think, act, and approach their own quests.

- **Inspiring others**: Just as explorers and adventurers of the past have inspired us to pursue our own dreams, your findings can inspire future generations. By documenting your journey, sharing your discoveries, and passing on the wisdom you've gained, you provide the tools for others to embark on their own treasure hunts—whether literal or metaphorical.

- **Shaping cultural narratives**: The treasures you uncover, especially those of historical or cultural importance, become part of the shared history of a society. They help shape collective memories and cultural identities. Whether it's a piece of art, a lost manuscript, or a rare artifact, your discoveries contribute to the larger narrative that informs future generations' understanding of the world.

- **Creating lasting change**: The discoveries made on treasure hunts—whether in the form of wealth, wisdom, or social awareness—can drive positive change. From launching businesses that help others to creating initiatives that support education or conservation, your treasure hunt can spark a movement that has a lasting influence on the world.

Through your discoveries, you leave a **legacy that shapes the future**, influences the way people think, and drives progress. You contribute to a world that is richer not only in material wealth but in knowledge, culture, and opportunity for the next generation.

---

4. The Future of Treasure Hunting and Personal Growth

As we look to the future, the world of treasure hunting is rapidly changing. What was once an exclusive activity for explorers and historians is now a **global pursuit**. With the advent of modern technology, treasure hunting has expanded into new realms—digital treasures, virtual reality experiences, and even space exploration. The tools we use to search for treasure, the nature of the treasures themselves, and the way we engage with the hunt are all evolving.

- **Digital treasure hunts**: The rise of cryptocurrencies and NFTs (non-fungible tokens) has introduced a new frontier for treasure hunters. Virtual treasures, online games, and digital collectibles are becoming some of the most sought-after items. As technology continues to advance, so too will the ways in which we search for and find treasure.

- **Space exploration**: With the growing interest in space exploration, new kinds of treasure hunts are beginning to take shape. Whether it's mining asteroids for rare minerals or exploring the vastness of space for unknown resources, the future of treasure hunting could extend beyond our planet, introducing a new kind of adventure.

- **The intersection of personal growth and treasure hunting**: In the future, treasure hunts will continue to be deeply tied to the pursuit of personal growth.

With the increasing importance of mindfulness, emotional intelligence, and resilience, the treasure hunt of tomorrow will be as much about inner discovery as it is about external wealth. The future of treasure hunting will likely focus not only on what we find but on how the process of finding it shapes who we become.

Ultimately, the future of treasure hunting will continue to blend the material with the personal. Whether it's uncovering hidden gems in the physical world, uncovering truths within the digital landscape, or exploring the mind and spirit, the treasure hunt will continue to be a powerful metaphor for **personal growth, discovery, and transformation.**

Conclusion

As we reach the end of this extraordinary journey, it's important to pause, reflect, and consider the deeper significance of the treasure hunt. While the tangible rewards of finding physical wealth are compelling, the true essence of this adventure lies in the transformation it fosters—within you and those whose lives you touch along the way.

This final chapter is about understanding **your role** in the journey of discovery. You're not just a passive participant in a treasure hunt; you are an active creator, someone who shapes the course of the adventure and influences the discoveries made. What you've learned, what you'll continue to learn, and where you decide to go next are all part of your evolving story.

---

1. Reflecting on the Adventure: What Have You Learned?

At every step of a treasure hunt, there are lessons to be learned. While the treasures themselves are certainly alluring, the true value often lies in the **wisdom gained along the way**. Each clue you decode, each challenge you face, teaches you something about yourself, the world around you, and the process of discovery.

Take a moment to reflect on the journey:

- **What have you discovered about your own abilities?** Perhaps you've uncovered hidden talents for problem-solving, resilience, or perseverance that you didn't realize you had. Maybe you've learned new skills in researching, analyzing clues, or navigating obstacles. The treasure hunt, above all, is a test of character and resourcefulness.

- **How has your perspective changed?** The hunt may have exposed you to new ways of thinking, alternative perspectives, and even ideas that challenge your worldview. You've likely discovered the value of patience, the importance of curiosity, and the need to remain open to the unknown.

- **What connections have you made?** The journey often involves collaboration, whether it's with other treasure hunters, mentors, or even the larger community of seekers. You might have formed new friendships, connected with people from different walks of life, or found deeper connections with your own family or local community.

By reflecting on these lessons, you'll gain a clearer understanding of how the **treasure hunt has shaped you**—and what it has taught you about your capacity for growth, discovery, and change. These reflections are invaluable, for they help you understand the transformative power of the journey, regardless of the treasure's material value.

2. The Treasure is Within You: Embracing Your Own Potential

As you continue down the path of discovery, it's essential to recognize that the **greatest treasure is not necessarily found at the end of the hunt**. It resides within you. The qualities and capabilities you've uncovered throughout your adventure—your inner strength, curiosity, and resilience—are priceless assets that will continue to serve you far beyond this treasure hunt.

- **Unleashing your potential**: The skills you've honed, the challenges you've overcome, and the courage you've demonstrated all contribute to a deeper understanding of your potential. The treasure hunt has been about **unlocking your capabilities**, showing you just how much you're capable of when you push past your limits.

- **Cultivating personal growth**: This journey is about more than finding external wealth—it's about deepening your sense of self and embracing growth. Each step you've taken has helped you discover something new about yourself, and the treasure you find along the way is a reflection of who you are becoming. By embracing your potential, you unlock the wealth of possibilities that lie ahead in every area of your life.

- **The true wealth of life**: It's easy to measure treasure in terms of monetary value or rare objects, but the true wealth in life lies in your **experiences, your growth, and your relationships**. The skills, insights, and confidence you gain from this journey are treasures that will serve you for a lifetime, enriching you in ways that no material object ever could.

When you embrace your own potential, you begin to realize that the treasure is not just something you search for—it's something you carry with you, a wellspring of possibility that is always within reach.

---

3. The Adventure Continues: Where Will Your Journey Take You?

As this chapter comes to a close, the adventure doesn't end—it's only just begun. The treasure hunt has shown you that there is always more to discover, more to learn, and more to achieve. As you look ahead, the path stretches out before you, offering new opportunities for growth and exploration.

- **Endless possibilities**: The lessons you've learned, the treasures you've uncovered, and the experiences you've had are stepping stones on a much larger journey. There will always be new adventures waiting around the corner—whether it's a new treasure to seek, a new challenge to face, or a new dream to pursue. The key is to remain curious, open-minded, and willing to take the next step, wherever it may lead.

- **Future hunts**: Perhaps this book has sparked a new passion in you, one that will send you searching for other treasures, both tangible and intangible. Whether it's another treasure hunt, a new project, or a personal goal, this journey has demonstrated that discovery is a continuous process. The thrill of the hunt doesn't fade—it grows as you move forward, finding new things about the world and about yourself.

- **The journey is the destination**: One of the most profound insights that treasure hunting offers is that **the process of seeking is as important as the discovery itself**. The challenges, the triumphs, the setbacks, and the successes are all part of the experience, and in many ways, they are the treasure. As you continue your journey, focus not just on the end result but on the lessons learned and the growth achieved along the way.

The adventure continues, but remember—it's not just about the treasures you'll find, but about the **person you become** as you pursue them.

Final Thoughts: The Treasure of the Journey

In the end, your role in this journey is much more than that of a seeker—it is that of a creator, a shaper of your own destiny. Every clue you follow, every challenge you face, and every treasure you uncover contributes to the **legacy you leave**.

The journey doesn't end with a final discovery; instead, it leads you to the realization that the hunt itself is a treasure—one that shapes you, molds you, and transforms you into someone who is richer in experience, in understanding, and in potential.

So, as you close this chapter, ask yourself: **Where will your journey take you next?** With the treasures within you and the world full of possibilities, your adventure is just beginning. Keep seeking, keep growing, and remember—the greatest treasure is the one you carry inside.

Made in the USA
Middletown, DE
09 December 2024

66550059R00084